70 Ways to Hear God

By

1UniqueWriter

CONTENTS

Introduction v

Hearing from God 1

    How to Hear When God Speaks 1

    Why You Don't Hear 2

    How He speaks to Us 5

Bonuses 99

Heavenly Notes 102

A Word of Encouragement 105

About Me 109

INTRODUCTION

Communication is a dialogue between two or more people. However, it is not effective if one of the persons is not listening or if someone isn't speaking plainly. Furthermore, it definitely isn't effective if a question being asked is not answered or if the message being communicated is completely ignored. Have you ever experienced being on the speaking end, asking questions, for which there is no response? What about the times when you ask God a question, but He says nothing? Perhaps, He's spoken, but you've misunderstood or missed His communication.

I know exactly how you feel because I've experienced those moments, too. It doesn't matter how many times you've communicated with God, you can still miss a word from Him. But why miss a word when you don't have to, especially when you really need it? There are various reasons why you may be missing His answers and messages; one of them being that you aren't communicating effectively on the speaking or listening end.

Desperate times call for desperate measures. I've been in difficult situations when I needed answers and didn't get them; it caused frustration, stress, and even depression. So, I understand how difficult it can be, which is why I'm sharing my personal experiences to help you discover and understand the following things about your communication with God:

- How to hear when God speaks
- Why you don't hear His voice
- How He speaks to us

As you learn these things, your communication with God will improve!

HEARING FROM GOD

How to Hear When God Speaks

Hearing God is not always easy, but it is simple. Sometimes, it can be effortless. Other times, you must prepare yourself and clear your environment. Just like in our earthly conversations, sometimes, there are barriers that prevent us from hearing and understanding a message; there are "noises." You may have some noises in your life that need to be quieted, so you can hear God.

Sinning habitually and willingly can also be a blockage. Repent of your sins and simply ask God to remove anything that may be obscuring your hearing. In addition, you must be submissive, meaning you need to open your heart and spirit, as well as, your ears to hearing Him. Cast all your own selfish motives and desires to the side and become completely open to God's will. You must be willing to submit to however, whatever, and whenever He does what He does.

The number one way to increase and open up the channels of communication is in one word. As generic and cliché as it may sound, it is what I've discovered is vital. As people, we spend excessive time focusing on relationships with other people. This is ordinary and understandable because we are human and humans make the world go round. If you lived in a world where you were the only person, I doubt it would be a life worth living.

As painful as relationships can be, they move us. But, how is it that during our detrimental times, we get so wrapped up in relationships and seeking help from people with no power? Shouldn't our most intimate, time-consuming relationship be with someone who can help solve our issues? Who can soothe our pain? Who can give us answers to our questions? Who can love us infinitely and unconditionally as we all desire? It's so simple until it's complex. Yet, the primary key to improving your communication is by improving — Are you ready for that one word? Well, the thing that may be holding you back is — intimacy. Even if you currently have a relationship with the Lord, how intimate is it? When you have a genuine, caring relationship with someone, you speak with them about everything without hesitation. According to John 15:15, the Lord is our friend and He confides in us — He will tell us things. Just as He confides in us, He wants us to be comfortable confiding in Him.

During moments when you can't hear God, take the time to improve your relationship with Him. Fall on your face shamelessly, until you hear Him. I don't care how long it takes. God seeks our hearts, souls, spirits and lives. Our everything. The closer we get to Him, the more we can trust Him. I guarantee, once you reach the ultimate intimacy with Him and experience communication beyond what you can fathom, you will never be able to doubt the ability to hear Him again.

Why You Don't Hear

As I said before, you may not be able to hear God due to blockages such as sins, selfish desires, and lack of intimacy. However, there are also times when you don't hear Him because He's not speaking. There's nothing worse than speaking to someone and not receive a reply. That will put you on the fast train to feeling alone.

I know what it's like to feel alone, especially when you are always misunderstood. It's even worse when you're always a good listener for everyone else, yet, it seems that no one listens or hears you. And if they even attempt to, you sense their hesitation to impart wisdom to you because they are intimidated. If you've ever encountered such a dilemma, I'm sure you've felt that you are normal and have issues, just as they do. You just don't broadcast your issues or consistently dwell on them and you don't wear your issues on your forehead or the affiliated emotions on your sleeves. Therefore, people don't "see" your issues or emotions, so they assume all is well. As a result, there's no one to cry to. Perhaps, people don't "get it" because you're crying to the wrong ones about your particular situation.

Moreover, there are times you cry out to God, and you know He hears you because when you intercede and pray for others, you witness changes and breakthroughs in their lives. But somehow, there seems to be static in the connection when you send your personal requests. Have you ever been in this position and felt like there was no one to turn to for help? This is such a painful and lonely place, and I definitely get it. However, just because you don't hear from God, it doesn't mean He isn't listening or speaking.

Even when we've clearly heard Him in prior times, I've found that there can still be other moments when we miss His communication with us. Sometimes, His communication is loud, blatant, and obvious and may even occur multiple times as confirmation. And then, there are times when you're confused and asking God what's up because the air is filled with silence. You find yourself going back to the beginning of time to make sure you've repented for every sin you've committed since you were in diapers. Of course, I am being facetious. I simply mean, we try super hard to make sure we've covered all bases. We stress our brains trying to analyze if there was a sin we missed and didn't repent of. Nevertheless, our sins may have nothing to do with the lack of communication.

There are so many other reasons we could be missing a word from God. On the other hand, it is similar to taking a test in school when the teacher remained quiet. It is not appropriate for the teacher to speak during the test. It is exactly what it is: a test. It's the time to apply all that you've learned during the good moments when the sun was shining and all was going well. It's the time to see if you can apply all that you've studied. It's the time to see just how much you truly learned.

Yet, I'm not here to scold you because I'm definitely just as imperfect as you. No matter how many times I've communicated with God, I still have moments when I'm confused. Just to be even more transparent, I'm still working on being stronger during the testing times. There are moments when God and I are in constant communication and flowing — then He goes silent on me. If He stays silent too long, I start second-guessing myself and then I have to repent, lean on His Word, and trust Him. I once heard someone use the analogy that He is like the GPS system. Sometimes, it will become silent and stop giving directions. But its silence does not mean the GPS system is not functioning or is disengaged. It simply means to keep going; you're on the right track. Nonetheless, because you are unsure of where exactly you're headed, you tend to become apprehensive and even wonder if the system has suddenly become defective and stopped working. But, if you make a wrong turn, the system will speak. Thus, I always affiliate the silent moments of

God with that. If He isn't saying anything, I trust that I am going in the right direction and I just keep going. I know that He is my Father and no loving parent wants to see their child go down the wrong path. Hence, I lean on trusting God more and more, even when I can't hear Him.

It's not always comfortable, but we must have faith, which is the evidence that the things we hope for will come to pass. I've come a mighty, mighty long way and I'm still a work in progress, but I know God will never leave me. He is my fortress and my ever-present help in my time of need. He is yours too. We must lean on His Word and trust it because it is truly alive. His Word, as well as His very presence, has proven to be true to me. I know God is real. He's spoken to me too many times for Him to not be real. Even when we don't hear God, He's still very present and very active!

How He speaks to Us

There is no limit to how God speaks. It can be via coincidental incidents, dreaming dreams, knowing knowledge, visualizing visions, and vocal voices, as you will read about throughout this book. God speaks through His Word, people, dreams, visions, numbers, patterns, things you see, literature you read, a "knowing" in your spirit, and many other ways. I'm not going to try to name everything because He is limitless. The bottom-line is that there are no boundaries to how God can and will speak to you. As you read about my experiences, you will understand that I'm not mighty enough to create such occurrences. Furthermore, if you've ever had any doubt about God's existence or power, it is about to be diminished as you read this book. I am confident that your faith in God will increase. You'll learn various ways God communicates and witness His fresh, new strategies. But most of all, this book is for you to improve your communication with God. As you improve your communication, your relationship with Him will improve and your hope, faith, and trust will increase. These are essential elements to experiencing a new, peaceful, prosperous level of living. To reach new levels in your life, you need to renew and reach a new level of relationship with God.

Sometimes, we make it appear as if getting close to God and hearing Him is hard. There's a plethora of misinformation that can easily create dizziness when you try to eat from everyone's table of spiritual food being served. Yet, all of the religious tactics won't give you a true, profound relationship with God. Those antics make you feel like you're never good enough or you're never doing enough for God. Needless to say, we don't have to do anything to deserve His love or even earn blessings and grace. But, there is one main thing we should do — believe! Believe in God, believe God, and believe God's Word. Without faith, it is impossible to please God and anything is possible if a person just believes. You need to know that God has a word for you. Have faith that you are capable of hearing Him.

Hearing God doesn't have to be tedious or ritualistic. You just need to become intimate with Him, which doesn't have to be difficult. Just be who you are; go to Him, just as you would anybody else. Yes, He speaks through people and the Bible, but people have perverted the truth of God and sometimes, you don't always understand what's in the Bible. However, these are not valid reasons to remain distant from God and confused about how, when, and what He speaks to you. The best message and interpretation of what God is saying is the message that you specifically get from God and interpret yourself. God deals with us based on what's going on in and around us. Therefore, the best communication you can receive from God is the one you get yourself. Others can be helpful, but you need to know and hear God for yourself. I pray that as you read about how God speaks to me that you will receive revelations about how God speaks to you.

1. **Driving Me Crazy**

I tend to make friends very easily. I even make friends as I travel and I actually converse with people from car to car via our driving. We tail, follow, and dash in and out of traffic together. One day while driving, I made a friend as I typically do. This person was driving the way I like to drive — fast! I figured I could reach my destination faster if I drove faster, which is just typical fast drivers' thinking. Right?

Suddenly, I heard a voice say, "You need to let her go. She's about to get a ticket." I would've thought that I was crazy; however, I looked in my rear view and side mirrors because I like to pay attention to my surroundings. I noticed a black car. It had to be moving extremely fast because I could tell that it would catch up to me within the next few moments. I slowed down and moved into the far right (ahem- slow driving) lane. My friend was then in the middle lane, getting further and further ahead of me, making it harder for me to see her clearly. Then, there was the black car, moving past me and making me feel like I was driving in slow motion. The black car moved from the far left lane to the middle lane and soon enough, it was on the tail of my friend. All I saw next were blue lights!

At that point, I was so shocked about hearing a voice and the warning actually manifesting in front of me, I started screaming. "Oh my God! Oh my God! I just heard a voice, and it said she was about to get a ticket and now she's getting a ticket! Oh my God! I can't believe it!" I must've ranted about that for at least five minutes straight without stopping to even take a breath. Honestly, I would've thought I was going crazy if it wasn't for my passenger confirming that the car we were following was indeed getting pulled over. I might've thought I daydreamed the entire incident. Lol.

Note: God sends warnings. Look out and listen!

2. Travel Light

Once upon a Saturday morning, I recall traveling. It was me and one other passenger. I didn't plan to be away for more than a few days, so I packed light. Nevertheless, after riding for about 1.5 hours, traveling was becoming heavy. I could feel the weight expanding and becoming heavier. As I drove I became more and more uncomfortable as the minutes passed by. I tossed and turned in my seat slightly. I no longer seemed to be traveling light. It was as if I was hauling a heavy burden.

Something began to scream my name. Then, I experienced a sharp pain. My bladder was full and heavy and the rest area was nowhere in sight. It doesn't seem like it now, but at the time, having to relieve myself was the most urgent and important thing on Earth to me. I was desperate for relief, but not desperate enough to stop on the side of the road in broad daylight; so, I started to pray. I prayed to God for a rest area. I know how this might sound to lots of people. Some may be thinking,

"God isn't going to just build a rest area within seconds for you." He actually could if he wanted to, but just how much glory could and would He get from that?

Nevertheless, after praying, an inner voice stated, "The restroom is going to be right up ahead." This might sound like a coincidence or a lucky guess, but it wasn't. How do I know? Well, when the Spirit reveals something, it's a different feeling from any other feeling. In fact, it's more than an emotion. It really is a "knowing." You just know. And by now, I'm sure you've guessed that after hearing the voice, a sign appeared stating the next rest area was within a few miles. I was relieved at just seeing the sign. I was most definitely relieved when I released and emptied the heaviness so I could continue traveling light.

Note: When the Spirit touches you, it is more than a feeling. The facts always follow.

3. Too Short

I'd just come out of a slump in my life and somehow, things were declining again. I was down on my luck and having a rough time financially, as we all do at some point or another. I had worked and actually made quite a bit of money. Yet, I was still hundreds of dollars short of paying a significant bill. I sold valuable items I owned for much lesser than I had paid. And I was still short.

Of course, I'd already prayed to God and was confident that He would come through for me. I'd already gotten extensions and the very final day came to pay the bill. When I awakened that morning, I was still optimistic. However, as the time passed by and 5:00 p.m. seemed to be getting closer by the second, I became apprehensive. There was no sign that God was still going to help, as I'd been believing. All I could do was keep talking to God to keep my head above the rising water.

As the time continued to speed up, there was a knock on my door. It was my cousin, with whom I'd shared my dilemma. I didn't tell her about what was happening to receive sympathy or money. I simply needed to release the pressure from my chest. Nevertheless, as she came in, she had a smile on her face. Then, she sat down and as she reached into her purse, she asked how much money I needed. I told her I needed $300. She counted and handed me a stack of money. And there it was — BOOM! Waterfalls! I was not expecting that at all. Yet, she told me about how the night before, the Spirit told her to give me some money.

After pulling myself together from the emotional release of pressure, I gathered the other money that I already had. As I counted, it turned out that I was $370 short, not $300 as I'd told my cousin. But then, I counted what my cousin handed me; it was not $300. She'd actually given me $370! The exact amount that I was short. She didn't know I was $370 short and neither did I, until that moment; but clearly, God did!

Note: Sometimes, we don't know what we need, but God always does. Just because you don't know how you'll get what you need, doesn't mean you won't get it.

4. Sister

I watched her walk down what seemed like a never-ending hallway. I stood immovable, in a trance, until she was no longer in sight. Once she disappeared, I was able to resume getting ready for school. I fought to hold back tears as I told myself that I was wrong and going crazy.

Later that day, my mom picked me up from school as usual. It wasn't out of the ordinary that my aunt was also in the car. But, why was my sister's boyfriend there when she wasn't? I could feel the stiffness in the air as we drove home. Then, all I could think was, "That's it. She's gone. She's not coming back. She's dead!" The waterfall of tears started, but everyone in the car was so in a trance that no one saw me crying. I wiped the tears and gathered the strength and confidence to speak, "Mom, where's my sister?"

The immediate hesitation was confirmation enough. "Um...she's not home right now..." Soon enough, we arrived home. My mom told me to put my backpack in my room and come back to the living room because she had something to tell me. I moved as slowly as I could. Although I already knew, hearing the words would ensure that it wasn't a nightmare or me losing my mind. As I went back into the living room, my mom really knew no other way to say it but, "She's dead!" *BOOM!* Immediately, I screamed and the waterfall of tears crashed through the wall of strength.

Earlier that morning, as my sister and I shared the bathroom to both get dressed for school, "something" told me, she was going to die. I was just a child and didn't really go to church much, so I was very unfamiliar with the Holy Spirit and how God speaks. For all I knew, I was going crazy. In fact, I sort of thought I was and chose to ignore what I knew and was feeling. Yet, I was able to tell her that I loved her that morning, although that had no effect on the pain I felt.

Along with the pain, I also suffered because I thought it was my fault for not saying anything. Of course, I know now that nothing I said could've changed God's plan for her that day. Or was it God's plan? Could we have prayed over her and changed what happened that day?

Because I was silent, I will never know. That's a prime reason that I cannot afford to remain silent regarding what I know about God. People perish because of a lack of knowledge, and I refuse to let anyone else perish just because I've chosen to be silent. I might have been silent then about God speaking, but since I am now familiar with many ways that God speaks, I will speak (unless He tells me to be silent).

Note: Silence isn't golden if God gives you the words to speak. Those words are worth a lot more than gold.

5. Peace of Heaven

I opened my eyes to a small figure lying next to me in the form of my son. At that moment, I began to cry because I felt selfish. Not that I would intentionally leave my child if I had a choice in the matter. However, it's like I didn't even know or remember that I had a son. Yet, upon awakening, all I could think about was what if my son had awakened to the lifeless body of his mother.

What drove me to those thoughts? Where exactly had I been that would make me not want to return? Well, this wasn't dreamland. This was one of those moments when you just know. Yet, I'm guessing I had a case of sleep apnea that night and had stopped breathing. Sleep apnea is just that: you stop breathing while you're asleep. During this timeframe, my sleep apnea had actually improved from the perpetual nights of waking up constantly gasping for air.

Whatever the case was, I'd somehow landed in a place that is indescribable, even years later as I'm telling my experience. This place was beautiful. It was beyond peaceful. It was like what the Apostle Paul described in 2 Corinthians 12. I cannot even utter to describe it. "Peace" does not even begin to explain what this place was like. It was too magnificent and it was as if I had no remembrance of my issues on Earth. This place seemed to be something like a garden. I was so excited, I said: "Yes! I made it! I'm here. I'm home." Then, there was a white silhouette that appeared. It had no definite shape or form to it. But, it spoke and said, "You're going back!" I pleaded and said, "No, but I'm already here. I don't want to go back." Again, the voice spoke and said, "You're not ready. You're going back." I said no again, but then that's when my eyes opened to me looking at my son, sound asleep next to me.

Based on how I felt and the level of "knowing" I had upon awakening, I KNOW exactly where I went. It was truly a place of peace. I've experienced peace on Earth, but it comes nowhere near to even a piece of Heaven's peace. Heaven is real!

6. Life under Construction

I was used to working at home; however, I reached a point where my life was under construction. As I passed through the job site (so to speak), I was hitting one bump in the road after the other. For some apparent reason, my employer's computer kept listing me as unavailable for work at home, even after making numerous calls to inform them that I was available for another assignment. Needless to say, I ended up having to commute to work. I appreciated maintaining a position that paid my bills and then some, especially after being on the short end of receiving, due to "construction". Yet, I needed to get out of the building any and every chance I could to talk to my daddy upstairs.

During one of my breaks, I was doing my usual. Enjoying nature. Observing the sky. The people. The environment. Walking and talking to my Dad as I often did about the path I'd been on, my current life, and my future. Then, suddenly I heard someone plainly and clearly say, "Well, what do you want?"

"Well, you know, I really would like to go back to working at home. That will allow me to resume writing and it's time efficient…" I told Him that working at home was the best fit for me for many different reasons. It would definitely make things easier for me. I further explained myself and headed back into the building to complete my work day.

When I got home from work that evening, I had a voicemail that someone left earlier in the day (but after the time I had my conversation with God). Lo and behold, the voice message was to see if I was available for an upcoming work-at-home assignment! Was the timing of that call a coincidence? I think not. The timing of that call was a God incident! He asked me what I wanted. I told Him and I received it!

7. Light in Darkness

For some reason unknown, I felt uncomfortable around him. There was just something about him that didn't feel right. My being about twelve years of age or so had nothing to do with it. Somehow, all I could feel was there was something off and dark.

Years later when I was age twenty-something, while visiting my grandmother, she and I were watching the news. There was a story about a woman setting a mental institution on fire. As more details were revealed, my grandmother recognized the woman as a girl who grew up in her neighborhood. Apparently, the girl went crazy after being molested and assaulted by relatives including her brothers. One of the relatives' names just so happened to be "that man" that I always had an eerie feeling about when I was just a child. I never knew he grew up near my grandmother's house until that day.

So, how did I have an inkling as a child that something wasn't right about this man? Never mind how I seemed to be the only child having such an uncomfortable feeling about him. The spiritual discernment I experienced was the Holy Spirit. It was God revealing the truth and shining His light on darkness.

8. Who're You Going to Call?

A relative needed a car and I truly wanted to help. After all, she'd helped me to get a car before. So, I had intentions to contribute money; however, life happens and I was unable to. After feeling bad about wanting to help and not being able to, I did what any other kind-hearted person may or may not do out of desperation. I did exactly what I had to do to get that car for her. I dropped down on my knees and prayed.

Have you ever seen the infomercial about the crock pot or some other cooking device where you can place the food in the pot and forget about it, without overcooking? It's the commercial when they say that you can "set it and forget it." Well, that's pretty much what I did. I prayed, set it in God's hands, and forgot about it. I guess it was easy for me to forget and not obsess over it because I trusted God. But then, one day (perhaps a couple of weeks after), my phone rang. I received a phone call stating that my relative had gotten a new Benz.

She didn't exactly have the so-called resources that you typically need when purchasing a vehicle. Yet, she called me and then I called/prayed to my Father and voila! So, I have a question for you. When you need help, who do you call? I hope not Tyrone. I hope not Ghostbusters! After reading this, you had better start calling Jesus on the main line!

9. To Be or Not To Be (A Leper)

What I know, realize, and recognize in my life, and the lives of others is that the things we speak actually manifest. It was the year 2005 when the doctor diagnosed me with an incurable skin disease. Ultimately, I had surgery and multiple outbreaks after surgery. There was nothing that could be done.

The suffering increased at first because of my mental state. I think the pain was more than it actually was just because I kept thinking about the nasty bumps, lumps, cysts, and ooze exploding from my skin. However, I became so devastated until I started saying, "I don't have this. I don't care what the doctor says." I would say it even while having outbreaks. I prayed and refused to believe that I had a disease. It took months for the power of my words to manifest, but I guess, I kept saying it so much that I actually started believing my own words.

Now, it has been over ten years, and I've been outbreak and disease free since 2006! With that being said, I don't care who says what, you need to be saying something different (if that person is not speaking healing, growth, and prosperity). Talk to God, repent, and ask Him to remove anything holding your prayers up. Forgive yourself (if applicable) and continue living your life. Of course, believe for the best and most importantly — expect it!

10. Wake-up Call: Sound the Alarm

Typically, I've always been a light sleeper. Nevertheless, I must've been deep down in the ocean. I could've sworn I was floating. And I could've easily awakened confused about where I was and what exactly was happening. However, I heard a voice call out, "We're going to go ahead and wake her up." The minute he finished saying the word "up," my alarm clock sounded. It was as if he spoke and then immediately hit the button on the clock to sound the alarm.

I know this particular testimony is extremely short; nevertheless, it has had a long-lasting effect because I am still here — in the land of the living! My friend, that was not a dream! I know what I heard; it was loud and clear! The voice that is — although the alarm was loud and clear too, like it always is. I'm sure I'm not the only one who doesn't like the sound of the alarm clock. However, I am and will always be glad to hear it and have it awaken me daily — an angelic voice is nice to hear also.

11. Showered with Blessings

I was a little frustrated, almost to the point of stressed out. I had been in the house all week long, without any outings whatsoever. So, I was looking forward to having a reason to get out of the house on the weekend, despite not having much money to spend. Nevertheless, I needed to replace a desk that I'd sold.

I took a shower in an attempt to wash off my frustration. Yes, I said it — wash away my frustration. Showers help to relax me. Bath time is one of the few moments when I can block out noises and slow down my constantly running thoughts. Water calms and relaxes me. As I showered,

I heard a voice say, "Now, you know you're going to have to do better than this. Push!" The voice proceeded to tell me that I would not have to worry about anything and that I would be told what to do. So, I said okay and decided to lie down after showering. As I allowed my mind and spirit to reach a point of calmness and relaxation, the voice resumed speaking. I was reassured that I would not have to worry about anything; I would have the money to buy the desk, as well as grocery shop. Then, this voice stated, "All you have to do is…" Certainly, it wasn't anything immoral or illegal. Nevertheless, I would like to keep some things to myself. Sorry. I love you, though.

The main thing I want you to recognize is that if you shut down your own thoughts and emotions long enough, you'll be made aware of God's. In this particular scenario, I could've continued to be caught up in my feelings and never-ending thoughts, but I made a choice. Yes, that's right. A choice. And just as I had the option to calm myself and reject being emotional and depressed, you too have choices you can make. Choose wisely.

12. Suppression

The battle with depression seemed to be never ending. Having many family members who had their battles with it, depression seemed to be an epidemic curse placed on our family decades or maybe even a century ago. Nevertheless, there I was battling with this ugly thing on a beautiful Saturday afternoon. I didn't have much money to spend, so I decided to make it a movie watching day. For a person with nothing special to do, I was enjoying myself as I relished the comedy and action movie genres.

As I watched television ever so comfortably in my living room, I felt something crawling on my face, so I quickly reached to knock it away. What I touched was wet. Liquid. Tears. Of course, I was confused. What was I crying about? I was having a good moment. There wasn't anything on my mind and on a conscious level, nothing was bothering me. However, it took only a few moments when suddenly, I felt pain in my heart. I honestly didn't understand how I could have nothing on my mind, and yet, be hurt and crying. Moments after feeling the pain in my chest, I became enraged. I was livid! How long was I going to have to battle with this? Why wouldn't it go away?

I found myself standing in the kitchen and saying to myself that I was going to start living carelessly. I would start doing anything. I would do evil to others and hurt them. Maybe, if I hurt someone else, it would somehow soothe my pain. After all, I was always trying to save and help others but it had done no good for me up to that point. As I thought to myself, "Yep, that's it. I'm going to start doing stuff to other people," I heard a voice say, "Now, you know better. You know that's not how God made you."

I looked around wondering if I was going crazy. But, the voice reassured me that I wasn't just making up voices or going mad. The conversation went on for hours. Then, I began to hear several voices praying for me. They told me that anytime I start to feel a little pressure to just breathe; they revealed that they're always with me and praying for me. "We love you." Is what they said.

There were many questions that I'd asked God in recent times. During those several hours with what I assume were angels, they actually addressed and spoke about every question and concern that I talked to

God about. On that particular day, I went from being emotionally bound to being rescued and "broken out" by what I never saw. With that being said, take note that just because we can't see something doesn't mean it doesn't exist. That's actually an excellent mantra to apply when exercising your faith. Just remember that there's existence beyond the obvious.

13. Prophesied Prophecy

A relative had spoken to me about her pastor: how God used him, and how prophetic he was. Because of what she'd told me, I was intrigued. I advised her that I wanted to meet him so he could prophesy on my life. At that point, I'd never received a prophecy, so I thought it would be interesting.

I finally had the chance to visit her church; however, it was New Year's Eve so there really was no time to be introduced to the pastor. Yet, I was fine because, at that point, I just wanted and needed spiritual food to eat to start the upcoming year just right! I sensed that the year ahead was going to be even better than the last. I could feel the Holy Spirit strongly as if I was sitting in the first row, although I was in about the seventh row back. Because I was praising and worshipping so much, I kept opening and closing my eyes. I recall seeing the pastor walk pass other rows to come to my row, but then I closed my eyes again as I basked in the Spirit. I heard the pastor's voice closer to me and as he continued to preach, I could tell that he was next to me. Perhaps, just two people away. I opened my eyes; his hand was on my forehead as he stood directly in front of me, prophesying.

I had to watch the recording of the sermon. The church is large and is televised, so luckily, I was able to review. I needed to watch a playback because I had missed the beginning of the prophecy, as I was lost in the Spirit. Anyway, the pastor's prophecy was accurate and the word of wisdom he delivered regarding instructions was also relevant. God gave me a desire in my heart to receive prophecy and he fulfilled it. Just as Proverbs says — God will give us the desires of our heart, meaning He will implant the things into our hearts that we should desire and He'll fulfill them. In addition, it seems I prophesied the prophecy.

14. Answers before Questions

Life can be challenging. As a result, there are many frustrating questions to be answered. How awesome would it be if you had answers before your questions ever developed? Extremely awesome, right? But, if you were always made aware that the answer was an answer, the question would never develop. I think that's why some events occur in the sequence that they do. Answers and questions can be presented to us in a manner that they're distinguished only in hindsight.

A few years ago, I was offered a job around April. I didn't give it much thought, but over the next couple of weeks, I was contacted regarding ten different jobs. I was confused and wondering why so many employment opportunities were coming my way when I was secure in my current position. Nevertheless, about two weeks passed since being contacted by the various employers. Then, unexpectedly, I received a notification that at the end of that business day, I would be unemployed.

I prayed and decided that I was going to be okay. But I wasn't confident that I was going to be okay because I'd been contacted many times in the prior weeks. I'd already refused those offers. Even so, I still felt that I was going to be okay. How did I know I would be okay? Because I prayed and I trusted God to take care of me.

The next day, which was the first day of being unemployed. I was celebrating, happy, blasting music, singing, and dancing. I was so joyous because I viewed this as an opportunity. It was an opportunity to vacation from work. I'd been working so much; I think God made me take a vacation because I would have otherwise not done so. Nevertheless, on the first full day of being unemployed, I received a call. By the time the call ended, I was hired! Just like that. It honestly wasn't even much of an interview either.

I believe that because I *chose* to trust God and was sincere about leaving the situation in His hands that He responded expeditiously. No one can tell me that God doesn't answer when you call! There's always a positive perspective that can be taken, even in unfortunate happenings. Having trust and faith is a matter of choice.

While I'm on the subject of jobs, I'll tell you about another incident. Unlike the previous example, I wasn't given the answer prior to the question, but I was seeking a job. I prophesied with faith that I would be contacted that particular week. I didn't prophesy based on any recent contacts or conversations. I just decided to believe and speak what I wanted into existence. And guess what? I was contacted about five different jobs in one week! But wait! There's more — a third example! This was also an entirely different time period from the other incidents. I knew the contract I had would have soon expired — as in a couple of weeks. So, while it was on my mind, I decided to pray for a contract extension. One hour after praying, I received an email stating that my contract was extended!

Note: Sometimes, what it takes is for you to pray and speak a word of faith and be highly convinced that the thing you speak is going to occur. It's cool to believe and expect, but you need to KNOW!

15. Shopping Grace

Do all women really love to shop? Yes, no, maybe, somewhat? Well, I'm probably the only one who is in the "somewhat" category, which is perfectly fine because it just further solidifies why I'm called "unique." I like being able to buy what I want, but it's only fun when I know exactly what I want and have a list. Control freak, I know! Otherwise, shopping fun falls into the "somewhat" category when I'm just browsing for anything and in that case, the internet is my number one favorite place to shop!

One day, I was browsing the internet for the perfect picture to finally put the finishing touches on my newly decorated bedroom. I had no idea what I was looking for and was perplexed (the spoils of joy when you finally have enough money to buy anything). I finally narrowed down my search and decided that I would choose between just two stores. I selected my colors and toggled between the tabs of the two stores as I browsed for the perfect picture.

"I love the sky and water," I started thinking to myself. Then, suddenly it hit me! "If I could find a picture with blue and brown that has the sky and water…" It was all of about five seconds after thinking that when I scrolled down on my computer screen and there it was! It was perfect: a blue and brown picture of the sky and ocean! Some of you may be thinking, this was a prophetic moment and perhaps, it was.

However, it was also evidence that God is listening, even when we aren't intentionally submitting requests and talking to Him.

There is absolutely no way that I caused the picture to appear like that. I can and will attribute it to the God in me. However, my question to you is this: If God can cause a simple request like that to be granted (and I wasn't even talking to Him about it), then can't He grant requests when we are talking directly to Him? Of course, He can. I don't think there's ever a time when He's not listening to us, assuming our hearts and spirits are in the right place.

16. The Package

I hope you read Chronicle 15 because this is a continuation of it. So, now that I've told you about how I found the perfect picture, let me tell you about when I received it. Honestly, the huge empty space had been that way for months. Everything else in my bedroom was finally set up and perfect and I actually sort of liked the huge blank wall. Nevertheless, I finally decided to give in and search for the perfect picture. Excited about filling in the empty space, I started wondering when the picture was going to be delivered. I retrieved the tracking link, but before I could actually read the tracking information, there was a bump against the door. As I approached the door, I heard someone walking away. Then I heard what sounded like a truck pulling away. When I opened the door, there it was — the package. It was only a moment prior that I was so curious about its arrival status!

This is just a simple example of how things are always working and fitting together perfectly without our efforts. We tend to want to know when something is going to occur, even though God already has the package on the way to our doorsteps! Sometimes, God wants participation from us and other times, He doesn't need/want our involvement, other than trusting Him and having faith. Searching for answers can have no influence on anything, other than increasing impatience, like when I was tracking the package. I knew it was on the way, but I was excited and thus becoming impatient, so I wanted the package when I wanted it. With that being said, let God deliver on His timing and it won't be a moment too late.

Note: Seek and you shall find!

17. I was Just Playing

Just as I do and don't like to shop, I do and don't like to move. I like the excitement of moving to a new place, but not so much the work it takes to get there. Every and anybody knows that if you have a regular job, you need to take a few days off from that job because moving is a job! If you didn't think you had much before, this is the time when you find out that you actually have a lot. I typically try to lessen the amount of work to be done by selling and giving away as much as I can stand to.

One particular time, I sold and gave away so much stuff until I didn't even have a microwave. In my new place, I decided that I didn't want to have extra, unnecessary things either. I still had moderate chic decorations, so I really didn't need much anyway. As far as not having a microwave, the oven was working just fine for me. However, my mom felt that it was absolutely necessary for me to have one. She completely omitted my refusal and one day, she showed up with a microwave. It was at that point that she wooed me, and I decided that I wanted one, so I gratefully accepted it.

I happily restructured my kitchen décor and made room for it. When it was time to test it, guess what? It didn't even work. I pushed button after button, but the microwave was lifeless. There was absolutely no feedback at all. Not a sound. Not a light. Although I didn't initially have a strong desire to have a microwave, I started to feel a little disappointed when it wasn't working. I'd finally reached a point where I was excited to minimize my gas bill and also heat my food faster but all to no avail.

I decided to turn it into a humorous moment and I started to pray over the microwave, as I laid my hands on it. Suddenly, I received the urge to stop playing like I was praying and to pray for real; so, that's what I did. I closed my eyes, put all jokes to the side, and started praying aloud for real. Then, I tested the microwave by pushing the buttons and of course, by trying to heat something. And that's when my sibling started shockingly screaming, "Mom! Oh my God! This girl just prayed over the microwave and fixed it. Now it's working!"

Note: You have power that you aren't aware of and therefore aren't using.

18. Catching Feelings

When I told him that he'd fallen asleep on me the night before, I asked him how, why, and what did he feel. He looked at me and gave me a one-word answer. "Peace!" is what he said.

The night before, a family member became distressed, distraught, and heavily weighed down by a recent mistake he'd made. He spoke about the countless number of blunders he'd made and how he was still making them. He was tired of his shortcomings and felt worthless. Clearly, he felt screwed up and that maybe, his life wasn't worth living. I'd never seen him break down and cry out so passionately and painfully. When a person is experiencing pain, I'm typically compassionate; however, I started experiencing something way beyond compassion. I suddenly felt an immense amount of pain in my own heart, as if I was the one in such emotional turmoil. As the pain increased, I realized that I was literally catching feelings — his feelings.

I desperately wanted him to experience pain relief and peace, so I hastily grabbed my oil and began to pray. I applied my hands to his torso with every intention to permeate him with peace. I have no idea how long I'd been praying, but I noticed he was very still and silent. I wiped my tear soaked face and began to shake him and call his name. He was asleep! The next day, I spoke to him and mentioned that he fell asleep and when I began questioning him about what he'd felt when I laid my hands on him, that's when he replied "Peace."

19. God Stopped It

When I was in my early twenties, I had a dream that an angel appeared to me and told me I was going to die soon. I was told I wouldn't live to see my mid-twenties. I was excited! Of course, by that statement, I really don't have to tell you that I was suicidal at the time. But after that dream, I knew I didn't have to do anything to speed the process and I lived with stimulating expectancy just knowing my suffering would be over soon.

When I was about twenty-four, my friend and I were riding in the rain on the expressway. We drove around a sharp curve, but then we were on a straight path. We drove through a puddle of water and it felt like we were then on a pair of skates. My friend hit the brakes and the tail end of the car started a slow motion dance. The back moved from side to side and then the rest of the car decided to get into the motion also. That's when the entire car started spinning around on the expressway. As I looked up, all I saw was 360 degrees. The sky was spinning in a circle! I recalled the dream of how the angel appeared to me. I leaned back, grabbed onto the door, closed my eyes, and said, "Father, forgive me for my sins. Here I come."

Suddenly, there was silence. I opened my eyes slowly, and it seemed that everything was still. I started looking around at everything in sight and checking my body for pain. I searched for evidence that I was a ghost. As I continued looking around, I noticed the car had stopped on a portion of the expressway that just so happened to not have a guard rail. Had the car stopped just a couple more inches over, we would've exited the freeway via the embankment and experienced a drop that would've guaranteed no survival.

As I sat completely up, I saw we were facing oncoming traffic. Luckily, the cars had ample time to stop before reaching us. People came to our rescue and asked if we were okay. I honestly didn't know what I was at the time. However, I was more rattled inside than outside. To everyone's surprise, there wasn't a scratch on any of us. After placing our misplaced souls back into our body, we proceeded on our journey. As we drove off, stiffened and in shock, all I could think about was how just before the car went tumbling over and down the embankment, God stopped it!

Note: Just before everything goes down, God will stop it.

20. Energy (Part 1)

Have you ever been in a room when someone walked in and then suddenly, the entire vibe changed? Everyone in the room may have been laughing and having a good time until Nancy entered; somehow there is a feeling of negativity. Energy doesn't lie! My admonishment to you is to remain cognizant of people's energy and the effect that it has on you. If you aren't being positively added to, I'm pretty positive that your positivity might be subtracted. Energy rarely stays exactly the same. If you're happy and a certain someone comes in, you either become happier than before or some of the happiness may decrease.

I *had* a friend who always had issues. According to her, the sun never shined, the moon didn't exist, all men are dogs, it's impossible for anything to ever go right and blah blah blah. I should've paid more attention to the changes in myself. I would speak with her and initially be happy, hopeful, positive, and optimistic. By the time our conversations ended, I would be completely drained. I tried so hard to pump her up with positivity that I was losing mine and exhausting myself. As time passed, her problems increased, and she required more help. Even when her issues were resolved, she still found a reason to complain and be unhappy and negative. When the jealousy and lies kicked in, I had no choice but to terminate the friendship. Plus, it felt like my optimism regarding many things was terminated too.

It's extremely vital to pay attention to how things feel in your spirit because God will communicate with you through it. Most of the time when you have a bad feeling about something, it's because that something is bad! Unfortunately, I kept ignoring the signs and patterns that revealed she wasn't a true friend. In fact, she was too hurt to even realize many of the unhealthy habits that developed out of her bitterness. But guess who should've realized the friendship was unhealthy and should've run before all of their positive energy got sucked away?! Yes, me! I know this example is not all that deep but every time God speaks to you, it's not going to always be all that deep. He speaks in bold, obvious ways, but sometimes He speaks so subtly that you can easily miss what is said. So now that I've given a simple subtle experience, let me give you something audacious! (Next chronicle, please!)

21. **Energy (Part 2)**

I had a different friend (than mentioned in the previous chronicle) that I would give rides to and from work. It was not a big deal at all, considering we were going to the same employer and we lived .25 miles apart. She was nice and humble; however, it also seemed like she had a dark shadow over her. There was a little bit of consistent negativity and cynicism residing within her, but nowhere near anything like the previously mentioned female. Because of that, our conversations became fewer and fewer, as I would deliberately play the radio to avoid the consistent negative energy.

My car was fairly new and had mostly traveling miles on it. If I can recall correctly, I think I had about 10,000 miles or perhaps, even less on my car. I'm not sure exactly when it started happening. All I know for sure is that it started during the stint that I would give my co-worker a ride. For some odd reason, when I would turn the key, my car would stutter and hesitate to crank. After a couple of weeks, I realized something:

The car never acted up when I was going somewhere, other than work. It only did this when I was giving this chick a ride.

At first, when I realized it, I tried to deny it; I questioned myself and thought I was tripping. But then, I paid extreme attention and started doing things differently to test my theory. When we got off from work, I would get to my car before she did, and it started up with no issue. So then, one day, I deliberately waited until she was getting in and tried to start the car—there it was again! The car started acting up. So, I tried my routine a few more times by starting the car before she got to it versus starting as she was entering the car.

Well, folks, my test didn't fail me! Oddly enough, the pattern was consistent and my theory was right. It was her! Every time she touched my car, either it hesitated to crank (with me trying a couple of times) or if it was beginning to start, as soon as she touched it, it would completely cut off. This female truly had something going on with her beyond the energy draining attitude. Not only was her attitude the type to drain your positive energy, it was strong enough to drain energy from my car! Lol. Is that not hilarious but tricky, all at the same time?! Never in my life had I experienced such an event of a person touching a car (even just the door handle) and being able to cut the car off. Perhaps, God felt I wasn't getting the message enough about hanging around someone who was draining, so He sent another level of warning! Lol. Just know, He speaks through patterns too and patterns don't lie!

Note: Sometimes, God's messages are not even as deep as you might think. They might be simply simple and a matter of you paying just a little attention: Enough attention to recognize patterns.

22. September 11, 2012

This particular morning, I was having a moment and was thinking, "I'm so screwed up, so who in the world can I help? I need to give up on trying to help others altogether or at least until I am completely together." Then, I started thinking, "What good am I? I've made too many mistakes, and I keep making wrong turns. I need to just give up all hope and don't try to help anyone else because I'll probably just mess them up."

Unexpectedly, I received a message that simply said: "Peace from broken pieces is an excellent audible." Then, the conversation took off from there. I expressed my thanks and admitted that I needed something and I was having a moment. Without me explaining the detailed thoughts that were going through my head, my aunt suggested that I help with a talk show. Then, she started feeding me with words of encouragement. With tears skating down my face, all I could do was shake my head, look up, and say thank you, Lord.

I cannot explain my emotions during that moment; it cannot be put into words. I could only think about how God knows that I will not place my burdens on others and although I needed someone to talk to, I refused to reach out to anyone. So He sent someone to me. When you feel alone, invisible, and like no one cares, it is tremendously amazing to hear someone say, "I am here for you" and "I love you." My aunt let me know she was there. God also let me know that He was there; He was listening and wanted me to know that He loves me.

Earlier in the morning, I was watching a sermon and was barely listening because I was wrestling with my tears and emotions. Yet, I somehow replayed words from the sermon in my head. "Glean behind the reapers." As I listened earlier, I was thinking, "Yeah, right. Who am I going to glean behind? I have no one to follow." And then the "aha" moment occurred: My aunt is very knowledgeable, skillful, and sharp. She is a reaper! Need I say more? God was speaking to me, even as I was wrestling in pain earlier in the day. He was working on things throughout that entire moment, which reminds me of another sermon I listened to that morning. I remember hearing that even when it seems like God isn't listening or doing anything — He is! All within a couple of hours, I went from sulking in despair and depression to a great moment of awe. It was possible only because I know how God speaks!

23. The Vanishing

A relative once said that there is healing in water and anytime that I feel sick, I should pray over the water and drink plenty of it. So, that is exactly what I did on this particular day. I felt a weird pain, so I grabbed some anointed oil, and I went deeply into meditative prayer. I'm talking about the type of prayer that takes you into the spiritual realm; the type of prayer that makes you feel like you are high on drugs! I anointed my body and my home. I prayed over the water and then I drank about 32 ounces.

I cannot even tell you when the pain disappeared because after praying about it and drinking the water, I spoke that I was healed. All I can tell you is that I noticed the pain had dissipated that day. The bottom line is that I prayed over the pain and that was my request. The vanishing of pain was the response. This is one of those cases when you feel in your spirit, and you just know that it was God. The more you speak with Him, the more you'll recognize Him and His voice. Although this case is minor, it's still an example that God is real and true healing can be received when you accept Him and believe in His power.

24. Coin. Me. Dollar.

I recall a moment when I did not have much money. All I had was a few dollars and there were many needed items that I was on the way to the store to pick up. However, I had to get just one more dollar to purchase everything. One dollar does not seem like much, but when it makes the difference between being able to purchase things you really need and trying to survive without them, one dollar can make a huge difference. I had just spoken about being short of money when my child said, "Mom, look!" On the floor of my vehicle, there was a gold dollar coin! My child and I immediately started praying and giving thanks because there was no other explanation for how our need was being met. We didn't try to logically figure out how the coin got there. The point was that the Lord knew when and what we would need and He supplied exactly what we needed at the exact moment that we needed it!

The real power that we are all capable of possessing comes from within; it is the Holy Spirit. I cannot express any further or deeper how real the power of the Holy Spirit is! As the power is constantly revealed, I know the Lord is real. I learn more and more to take heed to the direction of the Holy Spirit. As I reflect on moments when I didn't take heed, I realize I made horrible mistakes and allowed myself to be involved in situations that could have been avoided. I have often rejected the warnings by thinking I was just being crazy or negative. However, God was warning me but I took matters into my own hands and did whatever I wanted to do.

When we do not obey God, we can only blame ourselves. Nevertheless, it is not always easy to know if it is you or if it is God warning you. Therefore, it is important to constantly stay connected to Him. There's absolutely nothing wrong with talking to Him at any time and asking Him for confirmation. He will send confirmation. You just have to be open to communicating and willing to listen and pay attention.

Note: Pay Him attention and there's no limit to what He'll pay you.

25. Flooded (with Funds)

I had just started a second job a few weeks prior and things seemed to be lining up for me. I got dressed and just as I was about to leave, my car was under water! As I made my way to it and looked inside, the flood water was staring right into my face. It was definitely pointless to even try to open the door, so I went back inside and the outgoing phone calls started. I was upset for a laundry list of reasons:

1. My car was still fairly new and after this, it could suddenly become considerably old.
2. Although it wasn't my fault, I was already having to call into my new job.
3. Even though it was just a second job, I really couldn't afford to miss any money.
4. The emergency roadside company that I'd been paying wasn't going to tow my car.
5. Because they weren't going to tow my car, I then had to pay money to have it towed.

6. It turned out that I was parked next to a drain that contributed to the flood because my landlord didn't have it cleared out.

7. I'd already been having more than enough problems and just when I thought things were about to go my way, this situation was a clear indication that they weren't.

8. My insurance deductible was high, and it wasn't a good time to accumulate an extra unnecessary expense.

That day, I hyped myself up with all of those negative thoughts and affiliated negative emotions of frustration. Yet, what began as a bad day, ended up being a good experience:

1. My car was still like new.
2. I didn't lose my job.
3. My budget wasn't messed up by missing work that day.
4. I dropped my account with the crappy roadside assistance company and instead of giving money to them, I had more money to keep to myself.
5. I was able to get my car towed because I had money.
6. Because it was my landlord's fault, I could use their insurance to file a claim, instead of mine.
7. It was just a bad moment and this particular incident didn't mean I would keep having them.
8. I never had to pay the deductible to my insurance company.

I'm saying all this to say (or writing this to say), my mood was determined by my perspective. I helped a bad moment to become a bad day based on how I perceived the situation and thought about it. I guess seeing my car submerged under water sort of flipped a switch. However, it looked a lot worse than it actually was. To add more to my positive list above, money was actually added to my pocket! Because there was no major damage to my vehicle, and it just needed interior cleaning, I actually had an additional $500 in my bank account. Yes! I was basically given $500 just to be inconvenienced for a day or two. God knew I could use the extra money. Clearly, I could because I was working two jobs! I wouldn't have expected that I was getting money through being inconvenienced, but I am well with it. I'll take it however I can get it!

26. Computer Techy

I have a question for you. I might have already asked you, but let me ask again. Have you ever been in a room when a person walked in and caused the energy to shift? Well, the same way you can feel the difference in energy in that case, I can feel when there seems to be a dark shadow (so-to-speak) over a person. I don't necessarily have the exact details about what it is; I just know there's an unusual dark presence. I mention this because I had an associate on whom I could feel the "extra presence."

I had a new computer that I'd purchased several weeks prior. Although it was new, I'd already performed many tasks on it, so I knew it was working perfectly. However, my associate asked to use my computer, and I didn't see a reason to say no. An hour or so later, I went back to use it but something was wrong. No matter what I tried, I could not get the computer to work properly. I pursued a bachelor's degree in computer programming. I've also worked on computers for over twenty years. Therefore, computers aren't exactly foreign to me. It was frustrating because I use my computer, not only for pleasure but business too! But then, suddenly, I knew exactly what to do: I extended my hand, touched the computer, closed my eyes, and bowed my head. You already know what time it was!

It's funny how we don't remember to pray until we've exhausted and run out of all other options. It seems we have to become frustrated and desperate before we remember God is and has all the answers. I wasted time and energy trying to figure out my own solutions. When I prayed, magically, the computer was resurrected (so to speak) immediately after prayer. I spent hours "trying" to do something that God did within just a few moments. Along with the long (infinite) list of things that He is, God is also a computer technician. There's nothing He can't fix!

Note: Don't spend a lot of time trying to do what God can do in seconds.

27. Be Childish

The Bible says we should maintain a childlike imagination. So, I suggest you pay attention to the imaginations of children and take notes. In their minds, there are no limits. Yet, along the way, as children become adults, they encounter unfortunate incidents and misunderstandings about life, which eventually deteriorate hope. People grow tired and tend to lose faith as they continue to wait for things to come to pass. After waiting a while for wishes, hopes, and dreams to become a reality, many people give up hope and faith.

Everything we want is not of God and best for us; therefore, everything we want won't be granted. Everything isn't meant to be understood or accepted. Just release it and keep moving forward. Don't lose hope: If one dream dies, dream another dream. Let your childlike imagination catapult your faith. Faith works when you work it! Be positive. Believe!

This is what my child knows and has witnessed. There have been moments when his stomach would ache, and he would ask me to pray over it. It only took one time for me to put my hands on his stomach and pray, and have the pain dissipate. There were countless incidents that followed where my son would come directly to me to heal his stomach and even headaches.

Whenever he had a problem with his game system, I would hear a scream, "Mom! I need your magic touch!" By magic touch, he meant the power of God that comes through when I pray and touch his game. Actually, a few times, my son would touch and pray over his system when it malfunctioned. Even if he had prayed the last time and it didn't work, he would try to pray the next time before calling me. This is an excellent lesson for many adults who don't even attempt to pray over their situations before running to someone else that they perceive as having power. I'm not saying not to ask anyone to pray over you, touch and agree, but if you knew how to pray effectively and get God to answer your call, you wouldn't have to depend so much on three-way calling.

One key to getting my prayers answered is me having the childlike imagination to see prayers getting answered, even before God answers my call. Sometimes when I pray, I actual visualize the thing that I request of God. By the time your prayer ends, you should be completely persuaded that your call will get answered. If you're not feeling that way, go back into prayer and don't come out until you feel different. You should go into prayer one way and come out another.

Countless times, people have called me for prayer when they have the same power within. I don't mind praying for others, but I like to teach. So, if you keep asking me the same questions, either I'm a horrible teacher or the student is a bad one. Either way, something in the equation is off. I like to teach people that their prayers can work just as mine do. Of course, you want to repent and ask God to remove anything that may be hindering your prayers.

But, something I recall from many stories in the Bible is that when Jesus healed people and set them free from whatever bondage, most of the time, all He asked was if that person had faith. He didn't give a questionnaire of all the sins they'd committed and if they were up-to-date on tithes and offerings. I'm not saying these things aren't necessary, but what I'm saying is that having faith and getting prayers answered are not grad school coursework. There are times when you get an immediate answer and there are times when there are levels (i.e. level of anointing) to getting a response to prayers, but that's another book. One thing I know about Jesus helping folks is that Jesus had faith and so did the person He healed. Perhaps, those are ingredients to how my prayers over my son work — simply, two believers believing.

If a child can believe, why can't adults? I know it's easier for children to believe because they haven't been tainted by life and gone through the many trials and tribulations that break down and test our strength and faith. However, no excuse is good enough. If the children can have faith, so should adults!

28. Forty Days

After I finished my forty-day fast, many of my requests started coming to pass. One relative for whom I had prayed called me with joy and peace in his voice. Another received a job promotion. Others were moving one step closer to God. My hair was finally being restored after falling out so badly that I had a bald spot. My career was moving and excelling, I was experiencing a different adventurous outing every weekend.

I have different fasts that I do. During those forty days, I was on the Daniel Fast. Within the forty days, I decided to throw in an extra challenge: I went forty hours with absolutely no food, water only. By the end of forty hours, I couldn't eat, although I wanted to. I ate two spoons of something (can't remember what) and I had to force it to stay down with lots of water. My body was shaking and I was sick. I had to recuperate by sleeping and resting. Yet, I was able to maintain the Daniel Fast for what was left of the forty days. I typically like to fast to build my spiritual muscles and discipline against temptation. Although I'm bound to hear God at any moment, it seems like when I fast, I'm even closer to Him. It also seems like He downloads a lot more knowledge and wisdom into me.

Surely, God could've made changes in the lives of my relatives and my life, without me fasting, but I like to offer fasting as a sacrifice to show God just how serious I am about wanting Him to grant my requests. Certainly, such sacrifices may not be necessary, but it's just something that I have going on with God and don't mind doing for Him. Many people sacrifice things to prove themselves to other people. Are you one of those people? If so, what are you willing to sacrifice for God?

29. Frozen Still

Once upon a perfect day — well, actually it could have been perfect but it wasn't! I had to work and wanted to work in bed because it was cold inside my home due to it being thirty degrees outside. Yet, I guess I can't complain too much because I work at home, so at least, I didn't have to go outdoors and totally experience every drop of the thirty-degree weather. Nevertheless, it was freezing inside of my home, and I guess it was so cold that both my computer and cable box were malfunctioning.

I prayed and commanded whatever darkness it was causing my devices to malfunction to leave. I told them that they must go, in the name of Jesus! I, also, commanded the devices to work in the name of Jesus! I decreed that when I tried to use the equipment again that the devices would work. Yes, I did! I told that cable box, "Next time, you will work!" This might sound funny to you, but once you tap into the power of God, it's so amazing until you start using it on any and everything. Besides, when I call God's power to come forth, I doubt He's sitting back and laughing. In fact, I'm willing to bet you the million dollars that's going to hit my account soon that God is proud of how confident I am in the power of "Jesus." Clearly, I'm super confident in the name because I use it on small, tiny, minuscule, invisible, and all the way up to the gigantic, enormous, huge, "gi-normous" things. Lol. (Yes, I make up words and I'll use the power on those things, too!)

As crazy as it may sound to pray over and speak to a cable box and computer — Guess what? After I finished that prayer, when I tried them again, I had absolutely no problem. The television, cable box, and computer were all functioning normally.

30. **Driving Ahead**

I, often, dream about dead relatives. Throughout time, I've come to realize that they aren't always necessarily dead relatives. Sometimes, they are just familiar spirits. I've had dreams when my relatives have warned or given clarity to me about situations occurring in my life. I've also had dreams when I was so-to-speak tortured by those relatives. I remember having a dream of about five dead relatives who all sat silently staring at me. The look in their eyes and on their faces wasn't pleasant. What I know is the way they looked at me spooked me, and I felt disturbed in my spirit when I awakened. Contrarily, I've dreamed of all those same people in other dreams that gave me messages and helped me.

I recall a dream regarding my grandmother. It was actually a two-part dream. There was one part that revealed that I was to tell my brother something. The second part revealed my uncle offering to take my car so he could clean it and put gas in it. When I finally agreed to give him the keys and let him take it, my grandmother looked at me and said, "He's going ahead to prepare something for you." When I woke up, I realized she was speaking about something occurring in my life, and it wasn't my uncle who was preparing something for me. Why was my uncle used in the dream though? I have no idea. I'm not an expert dream analyzer, so I don't know everything about them; however, I know enough to grasp profound information. It's not always meant for us to know every single detail of a story and we never have to when God has gone ahead of us and made the way clear. In due time, He'll reveal every step of the way that He has for you.

31. Snake Patterns

Dreams are a major method of communication that God uses with me. During a time when I talked to God much less than I do now, He was speaking to me. I would have dreams about black snakes. Then, within a day or two, I would actually see a black snake slither across my path. As if that's not enough, I would then experience an over-the-top dramatic incident. It seemed that there was always another enemy of mine being revealed after seeing a snake in my dreams and also crossing my path in my awake life. It seems that God was warning me of the upcoming drama.

It never failed! There was never a time that I dreamed of a snake and then didn't see one when I was awake. There was never a time that a snake crossed my path and then I didn't have an enemy trying to attack me. In fact, there was a point when having the dreams and seeing a snake cross my path became so regular that the snake would slither in front of me, and I would just keep on walking, talking or doing whatever I was doing. They basically became like squirrels to me. You know, people don't pay much attention to squirrels. They are harmless, and they're just there. They don't bother you; they're just passing through. Well, the snakes never tried to attack me. They just slithered by. Before that time period, I was fearful of snakes, but I guess the dreams and constant meetings with them cured me of my fear. These dreams, sightings, and enemies fall into the pattern that I told you about (several chronicles ago). In this case, both dreams and patterns revealed information to me. I was able to monitor my surroundings cautiously because of the warnings I recognized were being sent via dreams.

32. Come Out, Come Out, Wherever You Are

For some odd reason, I kept awakening around the same time — within the 2:00 a.m. hour. It was crazy and almost annoying because I was finally gaining as much of a normal sleep pattern as I could. Plus, the nightmares were subsiding, and I would awaken feeling well rested and refreshed. Nevertheless, one Thursday morning, there it was again! There was something obviously demanding my attention and telling me to come out of my ever so restful sleep. Just as it was requesting that I come out, I wanted it to come out as well and leave me alone so that I could enjoy my restful nights. However, the thoughts started flowing and I recognized the pattern so I immediately conversed with God.

I felt that He was 100% behind this shenanigan, and I asked Him to reveal to me why I needed to wake up like this. Suddenly, it was revealed that I needed to speak with Him regarding a certain something — healing. I proceeded in the conversation and asked Him to reveal what I needed to do to receive healing. The Spirit revealed that I needed His truth and I needed to consult with my Bible. I was lying comfortably on the bed and my cell phone was conveniently by my side. Therefore, I opened my Bible app and started to read my bookmarked scriptures, but then I was told to hit the read button because I needed more than what I was reading. Why was I surprised to be taken directly to Matthew Chapter 9, where there are various passages about Jesus healing?

I was taken to those scriptures for guidance on how to proceed so that I could receive healing. But how did the Bible app know exactly what I needed? That's impossible, right? Yes, I know it is. It wasn't the app itself at all. Forget about it being a technological app. People get so used to technology as if technology provides all answers to all problems. We tend to get caught up in what God uses to reveal Himself. I get amped on the fact that He even communicates with me as He does, most of the time. Whatever the case is, it was technology, but it was also God's Word. A chapter based on healing being readily accessible was merely God revealing His truth to me in an intimate manner. The very thing that God revealed as a problem, within minutes, He revealed the answer!

33. Miracle 7

I had a conversation with God, the kind you have when you have been thinking and thinking and overthinking. I was thinking about the miracles that Jesus did, but I was telling God that I wanted to see and hear of modern day miracles. At the time, I had an issue; I needed a miracle.

Later that day, I was watching a Periscope video when the broadcaster spoke of a moment he had on July 12. (Periscope is an application by which the broadcaster livestreams and the watchers can type comments on the screen for the broadcaster to read.) He said 12, but he meant 2012. The ironic part is that my birthday is July 12th. When the numbers 7 and 12 are involved, God sends a message to me. Anyway, the broadcaster spoke about how he was on the side of the road with a broken leg and a bone was protruding. Nevertheless, he began singing a song but I cannot recall the title. However, he sang for about eight minutes. On the eighth minute, he watched as his leg supernaturally healed. In addition to this story being told of a miracle occurring on 7-12, the other ironic part is that 7 is God's number. My grandmother would always say that after the number 7, you will find the end of something. So, after the number 7, on the eighth minute, he received a miracle.

Of course, it was a miracle for him; however, I think it was even more of a miracle for me just to hear his testimony after I had such a conversation with God and my numbers were mentioned. Yes, God speaks to me through the numbers 7-12. Anytime those numbers appear, God does or says something extremely amazing that blows my mind. I know God was at work through this dude's message. God was speaking directly to me to believe Him for a miracle because He still performs them.

34. Disbelief Has No Effect on God

I sent a message to at least twenty people I know personally to receive feedback regarding a new project that I was working on. As the day aged, I rarely received any feedback, so I started thinking about how people rarely support me. My thoughts were about to take off in the wrong direction when I heard a voice. The voice clearly stated that I didn't need anyone to accept or validate me and that I needed to keep going, regardless of what people do or don't say or do.

About thirty minutes later, an alert sounded on my phone regarding a live Periscope broadcast. I logged on to watch the video and it was titled, "There is a reason why they don't support you." The broadcaster proceeded to expound on the subject as I reminisced about various accomplishments in my life. I thought about how no one supported me throughout the process and only showed up to cheer after the accomplishment was achieved. Then, the broadcaster stated, "You don't need anyone to accept or validate you. Keep going." Wow! She said the exact thing the Holy Spirit said to me. Everything she said during the broadcast was very relevant to the thoughts I was having just prior to her starting the broadcast. Can you say, "Confirmation"?

Note: You don't need them to believe in you. You just need to believe in you!

35. **Plain Vision**

I received a text from a friend. It was the type of text that a person sends first thing in the morning to start the day with a good deed, even if just to get "a good deed" for the day out of the way. Yet, the text was appreciated just as if it wasn't a group message and was meant for me personally. The text was basically referencing Habakkuk 2:2 to write the vision and make it plain.

I'm sure most of us receive daily spiritual, motivational emails. You know the emails that give you the scripture for the day along with a little explanation of it. The next morning, I received one of those emails. Guess what scripture it was? Right! You already know! It was Habakkuk 2:2. So at that point, of course, I had to be obedient and write to make my vision plain. I wrote my vision and prayed about it. One of the main things I wrote was — $140k! As if that wasn't enough, my cousin, who never dreams about me, called me to say that she had a dream about me. My cousin has many prophetic dreams and guess what? Well, I'll let you be the judge as to whether or not she had a prophetic dream.

She had a dream where she was basically asking me how much money I was making. And guess what again? Do I really have to tell you? All I'm going to say is — $140K! How, why, and where did she get that from? How could she be dreaming about that number?! I hadn't told her, at that time, I was making $40K and had asked God for $100K more! Yes,

I wrote the vision and made it plain to God, but then He sent confirmation and made it plain to me!

Note: Talk to God: He's listening!

36. Sleepless in Atlanta

There I was having another sleepless night. However, it wasn't the typical sleepless night where I got up numerous times. This particular night, it happened only once, but it was odd because I was sleeping comfortably and feeling well-rested. Yet, it so happened that I got up around the same time that I'd been waking up a couple of weeks prior, at the 2 a.m. hour.

The last time I awakened around that time, a couple of days prior, God spoke clearly to me and I thought I understood. Nevertheless, this time, I said, "Well, God, I guess this is just our special hour to meet and speak." Just as He directed me during our last 2 a.m. conversation, I went to His Word. Before I explain further, I had actually experienced a day of low energy, frustration, impatience, confusion, and had lots of questions; so, it shouldn't have been such a great surprise that He called me out of my sleep that night. I went to His Word and once again, I didn't even have to search; the scripture was right there. It read, "Submit to me and you will have peace; then things will go well for you."

Well, that definitely addressed the inner turmoil and questions I had from earlier that day. So, I had my instructions on how to clear up my inner frustration and confusion. With that being said, I spoke to Him about some things and submitted them to Him, which allowed me to go to sleep and give up being sleepless in Atlanta.

37. **Down on Your Knees**

My phone was on the bed next to me playing a periscope video. However, I felt the urge to talk to God about several things. I was sort of just going through the motions, sort of listening to the video, but in and out of conversation with God. Clearly, this wasn't an "on my knees" prayer. It was merely one of the moments when I casually talked to Him as if He's another human sitting next to me. As I was mumbling to God, do you know the broadcaster on my phone started responding to everything that I was saying at that moment to God?

It was as if she could hear me talking to God (of course she couldn't). On Periscope, you view the person who is broadcasting a live video, but they can't hear or see you. However, they can read comments that you type into the chat box on the screen. She couldn't hear me, but God was speaking through her to me LOUDLY and CLEARLY! I was touched so deeply that I broke down crying.

If you're holding onto some things that you're confused or worried about, talk to God. I promise you, He's listening. Stop carrying the weight. It's too heavy, and it's just going to break you down to your knees. Actually, being broken down to your knees isn't so bad because if you're on your knees, you're in the perfect position for prayer (as others say). Right? If you need weight lifted or a transformation, you can change your life by giving it to God. Submit!

38. **Lost in Atlanta**

Once upon a time on a dark cool night, I was finally done. I'd spent the last six days working tirelessly. I'd worked a full-time job and pretty much full-time towards my entrepreneurship. My brain was hurting and my mind was tired. I was looking forward to prying myself away from my desk and enjoying a night in the city. However, I would not have been disappointed if my friend had canceled our planned outing. As the sun's rays further escaped the sky's vision and the ray of lights walked away, darkness crept in and continued until it overtook all of the sun's light. Okay, so now that I've gotten the poetic version out of the way, let me just tell you straight up what happened.

Do you know how back in the day you played outside until just before the street lights came on? Right? You might have had a three-second grace period if the light did come on while you were still outside. Anyway, that's actually a good way to tell time because the kids should be in the house by then. Right? Wrong! For my son, he was extremely late, according to street light time. As I realized the time (which I refuse to mention) and peaked out the window to see complete and utter darkness, my heart immediately raced. However, I'm becoming better at responding quickly to situations with prayer versus being impulsive with immediate reactions. So, I began to pray. Then, I started to stretch as I talked to God trying to relax my body as I became tenser. I prayed and prayed to keep my mind on God. However, I started reaching out to my son's friends. Obviously, he didn't have his own phone on him. One friend, whom he always hangs with said he hadn't seen him and the other just ignored me.

I waited a few more minutes, but I knew I couldn't wait too long. So, I began to put on my jacket and boots. I prayed, "Lord, by the time I'm done please allow him to appear." Then, I went into the bathroom to pull my hair back as my last and final step before I was to exit. As I looked into the mirror and reached up to grab my hair, I heard: "Ding Dong

Ding Dong Ding Dong." I opened the door; I was so relieved to look into my son's face, all I could do was smile, although I wanted to punch him! I was too happy and relieved to be mad. Needless to say, just as I prayed, God allowed my son to appear before I could even finish getting dressed to hunt him down!

39. **Jump Off (Part 1)**

So far, we've driven down a pretty smooth road. However, we're about to turn onto bumpy terrain, so buckle up! Just as smooth and bumpy roads can cross, dreams and reality can cross paths. Has something you were experiencing in real life ever showed up in your dreams? Let me dig in further to help you understand.

One night, I was dreaming; in my dream, someone was banging on my door. They banged so loudly until I woke up in real life. I was so startled by the banging and noise in my dream that I had to go to my front door to see if someone was really there. Luckily, no one was at my door. However, I noticed that a mid-sized picture had fallen off my wall. The picture was hanging above a three-level bookshelf and there were three tall (1.5 foot) candle holders on the shelf. When the picture fell it knocked two of the candle holders on the floor. I had to pull the bookshelf out a bit because the picture had fallen behind the shelf. So, now we know what the noise in my dream actually was.

When I finally retrieved the picture, there was also something behind my bookshelf: something that shouldn't have been there. Something that didn't belong to me. Something that someone deliberately put there. I would've never had a reason to look behind the shelf to find this item.

Although I won't reveal what it was, I will advise you that I had to get rid of it because there was darkness attached to it. Praise God, His light reveals darkness.

Note: God shines light on darkness.

40. Jump Off (Part 2)

Speaking of pictures jumping off the wall, they actually jump off for different reasons. Want to hear a story about it? Here it is: I was having a bad emotional day and my body was exhausted. I felt that my strength was depleting as I was striving to do numerous things. I wondered how much longer I could keep up my busy routine and if God was even proud of me. Feeling mentally and physically exhausted, I finally made it home from work. As I entered my home, I stared straight ahead and couldn't wait to reach the end of the hall, so I could enter my bedroom and toss myself across the bed. Somehow, the picture on the wall at the end of the hall had fallen. As I picked up the picture, still intact, my eyes couldn't help but read it. "Strength and honor are her clothing. She shall rejoice in time to come… Many daughters have done well, but you excel them all." (Yes, these are scriptures from Proverbs 31).

On any other day, even with the way I was feeling I would've walked by the picture and not bother to read it. Ironically, I have various motivational quotes throughout my home as constant positive reminders in my times of need. Yet, I have moments when I don't even bother to read them. The fact that the picture was positioned in a way that I noticed it and then had a sudden desire to read it, is coincidental. Don't you think? Actually, I think not. The picture had good reasoning for jumping off the wall and the timing was perfect! At the moment, I needed to know what God thought about me and the picture jumped to advise me.

41. Open Your Mouth and Get Fed

Isn't it amazing how we can have no problem running our mouths for endless hours when we are talking to our friends, but when we need to speak to strangers on behalf of God, we get quiet? It's okay if you don't want to admit it, but I'll be the first to speak up and say that I can even talk to strangers all day. However, let the conversation become personal where I have to reveal my personal stuff and then see how I do. Actually, you know what? I've actually been changing throughout the last year. I essentially open up to strangers now and reveal personal information about myself. Still, I do maintain limits and boundaries. I've traveled a long way regarding that but I'm not completely there yet.

There was a time, within the last year, when God was dealing with me and admonishing me to open up and speak more about my personal testimonies. One day, I was out running and had just discovered the Periscope App so I decided to listen to the message as I ran. Why did the broadcaster start talking about not being ashamed to share your story? He spoke in depth about how your story will bless the next person. As I listened to the broadcaster's testimony, I realized how his openness was blessing me. The same way his truth was blessing me because he decided to tell it, I knew the same would be true for me if I would only open more, just as God was suggesting I should. Coincidence? I think not. Not only was the subject applicable to my present moment in life, it was applicable down to that very second. As I ran, I was thinking about sharing more of myself with others, so I can be even more of a blessing.

The things I've experienced were not just for me, but for many other women. Continuing to be silent can only hold up further blessings for me, as well as blessings for someone else. What good was all my silence doing? No one can hear my truth if I don't speak it. Right? What I've realized profoundly since I've opened and spoken up more nowadays is that a closed mouth can't get fed healing. You have to start opening your mouth! I'm telling you nothing but the truth. If you only knew the number of wounds that I thought time had healed, which kept reopening and resurfacing sporadically. When I started sharing more of my information with others, I felt a lot better. Somehow, opening up and talking more provided healing that time didn't.

Note: Your story is more for others than yourself. Don't be selfish: share!

42. If at First You Don't Succeed, Try Again

At any moment, I could have gone completely blind. I needed surgery and none of the surgeons I'd been referred to would accept my insurance. Who wants to pay thousands of dollars out of pocket for a medical procedure, even though you have insurance? Right? It seemed no one in the world was accepting my insurance. Well, not the whole world, but my world, which was basically the whole world to me! I became so frustrated and upset that I had actually given up and didn't know what was going to happen. I canceled the insurance because I felt I was paying the premium for nothing since no one was accepting it anyway. I stopped trying to find a surgeon who would accept my insurance. In the meantime, my optometrist told me that I was in danger of going completely blind at any minute. I was also told that if I started seeing flurries and if the blurriness worsened, that I would need to get to the emergency room ASAP!

As days went by, I had infinite thoughts. Would I go completely blind for real? That thought was hard to fathom. Would I have to borrow the money? Would I have to wait until I could afford surgery and risk going blind? Was this situation really happening?

I was told to try one more time. The next call I made was the one! That particular surgeon accepted the insurance. However, as a result of getting caught up in my feelings, I'd already canceled the insurance, out of mere frustration. This is an excellent example of why you don't make "emotional decisions," which are decisions made when you are highly emotional. Nonetheless, I contacted the insurance company to plead my case and request that my insurance be reinstated; all the while my sight was hanging in the balance. Because I realized it was God urging me to try again because He was working something out, I decided to focus on that fact. I decided to focus more on how God was my refuge and how I could trust Him, no matter how things seemed.

Focusing on God kept my mind at ease and gave me peace. Eventually, my insurance was reinstated and the surgery was a success. Although I don't have 20/20 vision naturally, without help, I am beyond grateful to be able to still see the beauty of the world. I understand your life may not be exactly as you want it, but things you take for granted have been completely taken from someone else. So, the next time you're tempted to complain about what you don't have, take inventory of what you do have. If you're honest, your list will be infinite, and you'll be writing it for the rest of your days.

43. Believe It or Not

I finally got tired of paying over $200 on a monthly basis to my service provider for cable, internet, and phone services so, I disconnected all and no longer had those services. I've always had a cell phone and nobody has a landline nowadays, anyway. Numerous options are available for internet service; therefore, I wasn't missing anything. As far as entertainment, I am entertainment! As far as keeping up with what was going on in the world, God revealed the news through the Holy Spirit and discernment. Besides, I wasn't where I wanted to be in life, so watching television was definitely the last thing on the to-do-list. Too many other things required my focus and energy.

One Sunday afternoon, my son and I wanted to have our usual Mom and son date time. This particular date would be Redbox movies and completely unhealthy food and snacks. We wanted to do so in the living room and put the television to use since it was only accumulating dust. So, my son put one of his game consoles in the living room and proceeded to hook it up. However, he was having issues with it. The HD ports of the television were shot and for some reason, the other ports seemed to be acting up too. As I hovered over the stove getting our food together, I started praying to myself. I asked God to fill my son with the Holy Spirit, guide Him and touch his hands so that whatever was wrong would be made right. After I said Amen, a very short period went by, probably about one minute. Suddenly, my son screamed, "Mom! I got it! It's working!"

I know it may sound like a coincidence to some of you, but the way my God is set up — I don't believe it was a coincidence. I don't believe it was God. I know it was God! We're all made differently, so it's fine to believe in coincidences. But, me — I believe in God!

44. Show Up and Show Out

By now, you know that I am used to multiple streams of income. I've always had 2-3 streams of income. I've had times when I've worked 2-3 jobs; 1-2 jobs and entrepreneurship; 1-2 jobs with overtime. I've put in a lot of work in many variations. So, you can understand how I can easily get used to having a comfortable amount of money. However, let me also include the fact that there have been many times when the bills were just as tall as the income. With that being said, it's sort of mandatory that I keep the money coming in.

Now that you understand the importance and my history of money making, so-to-speak, let me tell you about several incidents regarding overtime (O.T.) on my primary job:

Incident #1: I was hit over the head with an O.T. cancellation notice and the frustration set in. I had goals to meet and plans had been made. I was a little frustrated because once overtime is canceled, that's it: it is never reinstated. Yet, I touched and agreed with my mom in prayer and we prayed for restoration of overtime. I gave it to God and decided not to worry. I began working a second job, so I forgot about it. As far I was concerned, that was it — until I received an email stating that overtime was back on and this time it was unlimited.

Incident #2: It was a Tuesday when I received notification that O.T. had been canceled. I must admit when I'm able to work O.T. hours on my primary job, omg! I love it! I live very comfortably during those times!

So, upon receiving the email about the cancellation of O.T., I felt very disappointed, as you would too. In fact, I was so disappointed that I decreed and declared that O.T. would be restored by that weekend! On Friday, of that same week, I received an email that O.T. had been restored!

Incident #3: There was another time when O.T. was canceled and, of course, I was initially frustrated. I told God how I was tired of the up and down rollercoaster and how it seemed things would go right for only a second and then change before I could get used to them, even if for at least just a little while. Nevertheless, I decided I would not be frustrated and I prayed again (like before). I asked God to restore O.T. and then said: "If it's your will, restore. If not, I'm well with it because I know you're my provider." It was Thursday afternoon, and I'd already worked forty hours for that week, so I ended my work day. I'd only been signed out for just over one hour when I received an email, which asked if and when I would work O.T. that week. Talk about having a mind-blowing experience! God answered that prayer quickly! Had I not known my God, I would not have believed what was happening at that time was possible or acceptable!

Incident #4: I was just about ready to give up hope. Although I had a history of God answering my prayers, even regarding O.T., I still felt a little frustrated. How? You're probably wondering how I could easily get frustrated with such a history of God answering my prayers. Well, I guess I'm just like you. We all tend to get used to certain things (no matter what they are) and to some degree, we take them for granted. None of us is perfect, and we are all in the same fight.

Every day that we awaken, we must refresh our faith, our motivation, and our relationship with God. The conversations you had with God on

Sunday or last week are outdated. Therefore, you need to stay in constant communication with God. Even when you talk to Him on a regular basis, you must continue to work on your relationship with Him. With that being said, I can honestly admit that I should've had more trust and been more grounded during these O.T. related moments of frustration that I'm telling you about. If God is constantly speaking to you and you're still easily frustrated, you need to do more work. Looking back and meditating on these incidents, I admit that I was coming up short and needed to dig in closer, myself.

Back to the incident at hand, I prayed and prayed. Still, I honestly was just about ready to give up hope regarding O.T. when I received a telephone call — unlimited overtime! Do you know the adage, "God might not come when you want Him to, but He's always on time!"? Well, this was one of those moments. He didn't come when I called, and He didn't come when I wanted Him to. However, He was right on time! Wait! Hold on! Actually — Friend, things are always done in the spiritual before they are done in the physical. So, the truth is He did come when I called, not when I wanted. I just didn't know it was already done.

Note: Just because we don't see things happening in the physical, doesn't mean they aren't already done.

One thing I learned from these O.T. related incidents is that every time I say, "God, do whatever your will is. I'm not going to worry. I give it to you. I'm just going to trust you," and I genuinely let my requests go and stop thinking about them, He comes through. I don't even know why I freak out when all I have to do is pray. Friend, when we are well with God doing what He wants to do, how He wants to do, and when

He wants to, that's when He definitely shows up and when He shows up, He shows out!

45. Dreaming Awake

I'd been experiencing something very weird. It seemed that I was awake, but also asleep. More so, I was dreaming, but was somehow still aware of my awake presence. Have you ever been dreaming, knew you were dreaming, and tried to wake yourself up, but couldn't?

During this particularly weird experience, God was showing me visions of me praying for, over, and with people. He was telling me that He wanted me to start doing such. I told Him that I'd been struggling too much lately, and it seemed like some of my prayers were unanswered. I didn't want to be praying over people for nothing and giving false hope. So, I asked Him how I knew my prayers were going to work; He told me to just believe and pray.

My phone chimed and this was not in the dream. It chimed for real. At that point, I was able to wake up. I leaned over to grab my phone and had a message from my mother greeting me with a good morning text. In her text, she stated that there's power in the tongue, that I should speak in the name of Jesus and I'll receive. It also stated to remember that no weapon formed against me can prosper. How did she know I needed to be reminded that there's power in the words I speak? How did she know I needed a reminder that no weapon formed against me could stop me and the power within? Why did she send that text? We didn't have any conversations that would have motivated her to send that message. Still don't know? Well, I'll spell it out for you: G – O – D. Her text confirmed what God had just said to me in my so-called dream. It was God sending confirmation that my conversation with Him wasn't merely a dream.

46. Sister's Sister

I'd been thinking about my deceased sister, lately. I'd typically think about her and become angry about her leaving every time I experienced a new back stabbing situation. It's as if I longed for a sisterhood like the one I once had with her. When my so-called sisterhood with a so-called friend would go wrong, I would become angry because it was as if I'd lost a sister, again. Yet, at this particular time, it was just a random moment that she'd been on my mind.

I actually had an associate who reminded me of her. The associate and I were talking on the phone one day when she said my sister's name, unknowingly. Most people who know I have a deceased sister don't even know her name. Besides, she had an odd name. Maybe, I've heard one other person with her name, if that. So, it completely threw me for a loop when my associate blurted out her name. Although she was ranting and raving about who she wasn't to her then boyfriend, she named about three women's names and ironically, she stated my sister's name. I asked her to repeat herself and the names she said because surely I was just going insane and yearning for my sister's company just that badly. But, as my associate repeated herself, it was revealed that this particular time, I actually wasn't crazy or hallucinating. She said my sister's name!

That was simply a message, not from a genie in a bottle, but from a God in heaven. Again, you might be thinking coincidence, but how much more evidence do you need that nothing is happenstance? God was letting me know that just as my sister was on my mind, clearly, I was on His. God has many ways of comforting us and He will speak — you only need to listen.

47. Burying the Living Dead

A few days prior, I was speaking with a friend and she believed I never had a funeral to bury the old. So, she suggested that I do just that. Days later, I was informing my cousin of the said conversation and my process to release remnants of the past. The next morning I was listening to a sermon and the preacher kept saying: "You are healed from the past. You are healed in your mind." He also mentioned forgiveness. How did the preacher know that I was experiencing a moment when I needed to release and be healed from things of my past? I didn't talk to him. He couldn't even see me. He didn't even know me.

A couple of hours later after hearing the sermon, I checked my email just to find the scripture verse, Philippians 3:13. In case you don't know, it states, "This one thing I do. Forgetting what is behind and looking forward to what lies ahead." Again, how did this person know that I needed to apply this scripture to my life, at this particular time? The email wasn't sent by the preacher. In fact, this person didn't know me either.

With that being said, instead of waiting another moment, I went into prayer and told God that very moment was our funeral procession. I prayed aloud because it felt more intimate than inner prayer. I mentioned every hurtful, traumatic experience that had caused a root of fear and rejection. I named names, and I admitted that I was forgiving and FORGETTING those things and people. I also included myself because there were things I did that I needed to forgive myself for. At that point, I buried the dead and vowed not to allow it to keep living. I vowed to stop resuscitating. I vowed to bury the dead and not keep digging it up.

48. Being Abnormally "Cellie"

Let me start by saying that I didn't misspell the word "silly" when titling this chronicle. I actually meant to title this using the word "cellie." Yes, I made it up, but it fits perfectly. In a moment, you'll understand. Now, that we have that out of the way, let's talk about something that is going to make sense to you.

I'd been to the doctor and was told that abnormal cells were found. I had absolutely no idea what that could possibly mean. As if hearing the word "abnormal" wasn't bad enough, she mentioned "cancer" and stated it was a possibility. Honestly, I didn't care for her way of expressing herself and her delivery of this news. To be delivering even a possibility of such horrific news, she seemed careless. Needless to say, the way she spoke to me, I didn't want to proceed with anything having to do with a doctor. I decided, instead, to proclaim that she didn't know what she was talking about and the results were wrong. I just knew everything about my health was and is normal. I do too much to make sure of it. Instead of returning to her, I returned to my father upstairs and dropped down.

I prayed and rebuked that fictional news! I proclaimed that I was healthy until I got tired of saying it. Then, I went on living my life normally. However, I decided to visit a DIFFERENT doctor the next year. Tests were run again and voila — negative results! Happily, I told myself that I knew the other doctor was just a mean liar or God cleared up the abnormal cells or both!

49. To Be or Not to Be (My Friend)

I knew it was time for spring cleaning, but my closet and home were clean enough. Yet, there were other areas in my life that needed cleansing. I was already fighting not to be weary and to maintain my fervor for life. But I had some situations in my life that needed to be handled. So I'd been contemplating cutting some people off. I processed the situations multiple times, prayed, and ran information by a couple of people; it was obvious that my relationships needed to be cleaned up. Actually, they needed more than cleansing. There were relationships that needed to be deleted.

I started to struggle a little emotionally. I was definitely tired of going through the process of having to cut people off after developing intimate relationships with them. Nevertheless, I started hearing and seeing information from multiple sources regarding unhealthy friendships. None of these sources were affiliated with each other. Words spoken confirmed that the relationships I was contemplating were indeed toxic and cutting was the best thing to do. So God confirmed that those people, indeed, were not to be friends with me any longer.

50. Tune In for a Tune-up

I awakened feeling tired. I had weariness running over from the evening before. I was pressing through each day as best as I could. However, each disappointment seemed to be deducting way more of my energy than I could handle. My hope, faith, and strength were infested with extreme depression. As I sat, working and fighting to adjust my focus and faith, my phone chimed. It was a periscope video by which the broadcaster was about to pray. As I tuned in, the broadcaster started speaking about strength, focus, and maintaining faith. Did you catch that?

I was fighting on my own to adjust my strength, focus, and faith. And then, I suddenly had help! I didn't contact the broadcaster about my struggles, and he didn't even know me personally. He had no way of knowing what I was experiencing at that moment! Yet, he talked briefly about strength, focus, and faith. Then, he went into prayer and named and spoke to the exact things and thoughts I was having just as I tuned into the broadcast. Coincidence? I think not. Actually, I know not.

51. **Signs, Miracles, and Wonders**

There I was again, going through a sudden attack of extreme emotional sadness. I could be extremely happy one minute, and then extremely sad the next, without warning. Nothing would even have to happen for the emotional shift to occur. So, I couldn't help but to ask God what was wrong with me and why I kept having emotional struggles. I started asking long hard questions because I was tired of the repeated cycle. I was genuinely ready to get off of the merry go round.

My phone chimed to inform me that a live Periscope broadcast was occurring. The broadcast just so happened to be about healing from strongholds and curses. There were various scriptures given. I decided to add them to my list of affirmations, which I speak over my life. Among those scriptures, the broadcaster recommended Isaiah 53:5. Ironically, I'd just studied this scripture as I sat at my computer. Then, for whatever reason, I decided to open the Bible App on my phone. Guess what the day's recommended scripture was? Of course, it was Isaiah 53:5! In addition, the day prior, I received an email with the scripture Philippians 3:13 stating, "This one thing I do, forgetting what lies behind and pressing forward to what lies ahead." Then, I realized that during the previous few days, there were various signs regarding breaking free and being healed from the past and curses. Signs and wonders were definitely around me, so I knew miracles were occurring too.

It's crazy how I awakened that day feeling like I wasn't moving forward and making much progress. Ironically, I kept seeing messages on Instagram, various memes, and captions stating that speed doesn't matter as long as I keep moving forward. I wasn't even on Instagram long enough to see the number of memes and captions, I kept seeing, that were all talking about this. Seeing so many of those posts really helped because I'd been feeling like nothing progressive was happening. As far as forward movement in my (mostly writing) life was concerned, I was either stagnant or moving extremely slowly. Yet, I was two chronicles from finishing the book that you're reading, working on other literary projects, plus having a full-time job.

Sometimes, we need to stop, recognize, and appreciate our own efforts and progress, even if there's very little of it. In retrospect, I can see where I was making progress but I just wasn't where I wanted to be. Moreover, my focus was too far ahead, rather than being where it needed to be, which is where I was. I was also second-guessing myself about writing, even though it's something I've done effortlessly since childhood. For some reason, I had moments of thinking the reason for things moving so slowly was that perhaps, I wasn't doing the right thing. Perhaps, writing just wasn't my forte. I'm sure you can agree with me on just how flawed my thinking was when my focus was off. Our focus is a lot more accurate when we choose to zoom in on the signs, miracles, and wonders that God places right within clear view.

52. Good isn't God

I had just written articles and went through a process of deliverance after being fooled into doing things that were leading me on a path to hell. Ironically, I was doing things in an attempt to please God and walk in my God-given path and purpose. Somehow, I was tricked and started mistaking the wrong voices for the Holy Spirit. Unless you've experienced this, you won't understand. The voice I heard sounded just like the Holy Spirit, which I know the sound of without a doubt. Nevertheless, I'd been doing things that opened a gateway for demons and the Devil. Of course, this was done unknowingly. I stopped hearing the real voice of God. I would ask God questions and couldn't seem to get many answers. When I did get answers, things weren't going the way they should've if it was really God. I was so confused. There were times when I asked questions and got confirmation about different things; however, it was not of God.

Just as I was finally delivered, I watched a Periscope video of an apostle who described everything I'd experienced. He stated there's a counterfeit, the very thing I'd recently written an article about. I wrote the article due to my experience of being fooled by the counterfeit. As the apostle continued, he started confirming every single thing I'd experienced. He also spoke about favor and how we need discernment. We will be tested by the counterfeit and as stated by the apostle, 9/10 times, many won't know. Yet, when you're tested by the counterfeit, favor is coming.

There were many great points that were made about how people are able to be tricked by the counterfeit. He mentioned people being tricked because of a spirit of rejection, which God recently revealed was upon me and that was part of my issue in my relationships with people and me being overly nice. People who are still impacted by rejection tend to do things just to be accepted. The man of God talked about the Devil tricking people with things, such as being prosperous or making you think he wants you to experience love, peace, and happiness. He will also open doors and allow your desires to manifest. People then assume they are receiving blessings from God. That's how the Devil lures you in, which is the same thing I'd written in that article mentioned earlier. God used the apostle's voice to confirm how I'd been under attack and influenced by the counterfeit. It's not always easy to distinguish the real from fake because we tend to get caught up in what appears to be good. Yet, as I've heard many times, everything that's good isn't God.

53. Fast Healing

And again, there I was in an excessive depression type of moment. The kind where you tend to experience extreme, over-the-top, excessive sadness. Many times, an episode occurs unexpectedly and there may or May not be a specific, direct reason triggering it. There I was, suddenly sad. I was crying, feeling inner pain and trying to figure out why and if there was a logical reason. Luckily, it wasn't like any of the other extreme episodes. Yet, I was trying to figure out the reason for my then emotional state. After trying to figure the reason and not coming up with one, I started speaking against it.

I declared how God said that particular season and constant battles of depression were over. Suddenly, I had the idea to fast. I would fast the next day for seven hours and not consume any food or drink, but water. This was part of an act of faith to rebuke whatever curse, illness, and demon was trying to attack. I decreed and declared healing in my spirit, mind, and body over any demonic attack that was upon me.

The next day, I received two scriptures from different sources:

- *"Is not this the kind of fasting I have chosen: to loose the chains of injustice and untie the cords of the yoke, to set the oppressed free and break every yoke?"* Isaiah 58:6. How did this person know that I went on a fast for this reason? How did I get this scripture AFTER deciding to fast to loose the curse? How did the sender know to send me such a prophetic scripture? I didn't even know this person and they didn't even know my situation.

- *"But he was pierced for our transgressions, he was crushed for our iniquities; the punishment that brought us peace was on him, and by his wounds we are healed."* Isaiah 53:5. The same questions apply regarding the sender of this scripture. How did this person know to send such a prophetic scripture regarding healing? Just like the other sender, I didn't know this person and they didn't know my situation.

What I know is that if the Devil can keep me depressed, my motivation and strength will be depleted so I can't feed the hungry who are in need of the Bread of Life. The hungry need what God has put inside of me. If I am depressed, I can't clothe and cover the naked. How can I pray to cover others if my prayer life is hanging in the balance and my prophetic tongue has gone lazy due to depression? I can't.

Note: If the Devil can stop you, he can stop others from getting what they need.

54. Pass Fail

The attack came from nowhere. I suddenly felt overwhelmed and sad. I started thinking about how I had so many ideas and so much to do. I started talking to God, telling Him how much I needed Him. I spoke with Him about various topics, including business ventures. I'd already done many things and even owned businesses: contract business administration, modeling, network marketing, vending machines, real estate investments, and the list goes on and on. I still felt like a failure. I told God that if I fail at one more thing, I'm going to just give up. I proceeded to tell Him how tired I was and perhaps, I shouldn't even bother trying much more. When I told Him I felt like a failure, I heard a voice say that there were no failures, only lessons; I was reminded of a time when I was about to quit something. During that time, I decided to give something one last try and that last try made all the difference — I got what I needed.

As I talked to God and fought to rebuild my energy and positive mindset, I decided to scroll through Facebook. Surprisingly, there was a post stating that anything God touches cannot fail, including me. Then, I scrolled to the next post, which encouraged me to never stop dreaming because life can go from zero to one hundred real quick. Then, minutes later, I received an email that asked a question about why throw in the towel on an idea, dream or vision. The email also addressed not knowing where to start, how to get self out there, how to charge my worth, and how excuses are death. To see all of these pertinent messages within the same time period was simply amazing. Was it a coincidence? I'm just going to leave that question right here. Reread this chronicle if you need to and let me know what you think. Email me or even post a message on a social media account. What do you think?

Note: Even if you "fail," you can still excel "pass" it.

55. Focused with a Blurry Vision

The entire week prior, the message to stay focused consistently came through. I heard the Spirit say to delete distractions and stay focused. A couple of motivational speakers and life coaches spoke that same word. Within the same week, I watched "War Room" for the first time and the older lady said to remove distractions and stay focused.

Despite receiving numerous motivational messages, the next week, I was having moments of frustration and impatience. I was ready for some things to come to fruition. I was so frustrated that I completely lost focus of the prior week's profound messages. It seemed that I completely forgot to overlook distractions and remain focused.

I was working when my phone chimed; I looked to see that I had a motivational message via an app that I had subscribed to. The message read, "You can't think you'll make a difference and not deal with distractions. Stay focused!" There the message was again! At that time, I was definitely distracted and buried in frustration. In one moment, I even felt like I didn't want to try to make a difference. My impatience and frustration were enough to just throw in the towel. Nevertheless, the message came through to remind me that I was allowing myself to become distracted and lose focus.

To top off the long day I'd had, my son rang the doorbell after school, and I was wondering why he didn't use his key to get in. I opened the door, his hands were behind his back and out of the blue, he pulled out some flowers. He said that as he walked by some flowers, I crossed his mind and he just felt the need to get flowers to cheer me up. How did he know I needed to be cheered up after a long day? I hadn't shown any frustration or any other negative emotions that morning when he left for school. In fact, I was cheerful and happy, just as the majority of my mornings start. So, what made him feel that I needed to be cheered up? All of these signs and wonders coming to me at such relevant times can't just be coincidental. Can they? What do you think?

Note: When frustration blurs your vision, adjust your focus. It's not your sight, it's what you're looking at.

56. Hold On When On-Call

I was feeling mentally, emotionally, physically, and spiritually drained. I received one of my usual daily spiritual emails: "Weeping may last through the night, but joy comes with the morning" (Psalm 30:5 NLT). I scanned it, even though I was tired of praying, hoping, and waiting. As I read, I thought "blah, blah, blah."

A few hours later, I received another email to call a line for a motivational teleconference, and I did. People discussed how the journey gets longer and harder and how distractions also occur. In addition, the speaker talked about being called to endure and holding on during good and bad seasons. Then, guess what scripture he quoted? I'll wait... By now, you should be able to pass any and every pop quiz that I throw your way. Surely, you guessed it correctly. He quoted the scripture discussed above: Psalm 30:5. Although, I was in a moment when I was even questioning my spirituality, both the email and conference call were messages from God. He was sending messages to strengthen me. Coincidence? It's only a coincidence if you spell the word "coincidence" as G – O – D.

57. Bless Mind

I'd been working 7 days a week, 55-60 hours on my full-time job and 6-8 hours on my business. The exhaustion was starting to settle. One morning, I was logging into software for my job when I had to reset my password. I knew what I was typing; however, when I tried to log into an additional session, I couldn't get the password together. I was tired, but I couldn't have been that tired. I even recorded the password but every time I typed it, it was wrong. To avoid being locked out of the system, I logged off and on at least ten times.

It was too early in the morning for this type of activity and confusion, so I stopped trying to access an additional session for about one hour. Then, I decided to retry. Just before I tried again, I stopped to pray and asked God to bless the system and my mind this time, as I logged in. Sounds funny? Well, how many times have you tried to do something small on your own and you were "never" successful in your attempts because you "never" prayed about it? Ok, I'll admit, it is a little funny, but at least I prayed. I just don't think you can ever pray too much.

Are you still laughing at me? Well, guess what? I logged in slowly so I was mindful of what I typed and voila, I was in!! Coincidence? I think not. I asked God to bless my mind, and He did just that. It might sound a little funny, but God truly wants to be involved in even the smallest details and confusion of our lives. Don't believe me? Just ask. Ask Him for whatever — any small thing, any big thing. Trust me. "Won't He do it?" Yes, He will!

58. Wondering Sign

This particular day started out as a day of low energy, low self-esteem, and low confidence. I woke up thinking of the negative feedback I'd received regarding my business venture. I'd been working tirelessly on it, and I felt a little discouraged. It seemed that I was getting no closer to being successful and producing sales. I was still working at trying to perfect the website. Surely, the website was holding me back.

But then it was like the day restarted for me. It began with a message from God about keeping my fire lit. The word was sent through a prophet. He said God was getting ready to do something so I should remain passionate. I was stoked by that message, but still, not at a level of complete positive energy. As instructed by the prophet, I declared it would be the best day I've had in a long time and went into prayer, praise, and worship. I'd been going for at least one hour and listening to a praise sermon when suddenly, I felt something take over.

I could actually feel something permeating my body. I became dizzy and immediately felt like I was high. There was only one thing for me to do — lean back and let it have its way. Needless to say, it definitely was the best day I'd had in an extremely long time. I'd been declaring that miracles, signs, and wonders follow me all the days of my life. That particular day, it was no wonder that God sent me a sign!

59. Unique Wondering in Wonderland

I'd been pondering some things and foolishly trying to think about them with my common sense instead of just asking God: Why would God put that tree there? He knows everything. He knew they would eat from it. These were the words in my thoughts that were getting away from me. In case you can't tell, I'd been reading the Bible — the book of Genesis.

That same day, a live Periscope video came on and the broadcaster just so happened to be talking about how God gives us a choice so we can serve Him genuinely. By now, I shouldn't have to tell you that I never presented my thoughts and questions to the broadcaster. So, for her to broadcast and provide answers to my questions, it must have been a coincidence. Right?

Later that day, I watched a movie and a character just so happened to ask why God lets bad things happen and doesn't just destroy the Devil. This was so in alignment with my lines of questioning. I also started thinking about how good people suffer. Luckily for me, the movie facilitated various revelations: The Devil works to make it look like choosing God is choosing suffering. In addition, the Devil makes things look comfortable to deceive and trick people into serving Him. He will dress things up, but there's suffering beneath the blurred lines.

Although I was getting lost in a sea of emotions and wondering within my own mind, God sent resources to provide clear answers. God will answer questions, even without you asking Him. Of course, I definitely don't advise it. Besides, why give yourself a headache and get tossed up and around by a mental maze when God can reveal the straight path through? What good does it serve you to get lost and suffer alone through a journey of a confusing mental maze? Don't feel bad if you've ever wondered yourself into a wonderland. Even with gifts, sometimes, I become too fleshly and confused myself, as you can see. This chronicle is a primary example of why we should ***seek God and not lean on our own understanding***. We can confuse ourselves and situations and reap confusion in our lives.

60. IG Stories

I was having another typical day of sitting and wondering myself into wonderland. I was wondering if things I do actually help people, despite past encounters and being told that they do. I guess I just needed a reminder. At this particular moment, I was wondering if my Instagram posts even make a difference or if people subconsciously double click as they speedily scroll. Then, I received an Instagram message saying how it was becoming creepy that my posts were always relevant. This particular follower stated that my posts seemed to always be speaking directly to him. Apparently, my posts would be on-time words and responses to his current situations. Yet, his response to me was a response to my wondering.

61. Sleep Walking

I love having the type of friends who have a life. The type of friends who don't have time to call you about any and everything. The type of friends who try to solve their own issues before they try to involve everybody under the moon, meanwhile excluding God from the process. Although I had a group of friends that I spent several years hanging with, all four of us have pretty much separated and gone our own ways. All four of us are no longer able to keep up with each other and keep our "gang" together. Nevertheless, someone talks to somebody, somehow, every now and then.

Months had gone by since I'd spoken to one of those friends. So, when I had a dream about her, I was a little confused. We also lived in different states; hence, we weren't going to run into each other anytime soon. Nevertheless, in the dream, she was in my community strolling when a dog suddenly attacked her and started eating her alive. I watched as it happened, but it's like I was only there in the spirit; therefore, I wasn't able to stop the attack. This was actually the second dream that I had about her that night. The dream I had before occurred at a funeral. It was her funeral. Many of us spoke about the good times and various accounts we had with her. Needless to say, I woke up that day extremely bothered by those dreams.

I pondered on those dreams for a couple of days, until I couldn't take it anymore. I reached out to one of our other friends from the "gang" to see if they'd spoken recently. Because they lived in the same city and were meeting frequently at one point, I thought I might've been able to gain some "inside" information about how the friend I dreamed about was doing. I, also, wanted to discuss the dreams to see what our other friend thought about them. That phone call led me to a dead end and I still didn't know how my friend was doing, so I reached out to her to find out.

I could tell that something wasn't right. Although she didn't give me every bit of detailed information regarding everything that was happening, I knew the main thing I needed to know. Just as my dream had revealed, something was eating her alive and felt like it was going to kill her. The purpose of God revealing the information to me via a dream may have been because she was right on the edge of giving up completely. Perhaps, she needed someone to check on her. That part, I'll never know because I didn't, nor am I going to, ask. All I knew was that she needed prayer! After our discussion, I did exactly as I needed to — I prayed!

Note: Not only does God speak to us regarding us, but He gives us knowledge and wisdom for others, too.

62. I Say Uhhhhh…

I've recently embarked and stumbled onto a new path (so to speak). God is speaking to me via the same method in a different way. Sounds confusing but stick with me and I'll clear it up.

God places adequate scriptures before me and He also sends messages via dreams, but recently He's combined those two methods of communication. Yes, you read it correctly. It happened unexpectedly and one week, I had a couple of dreams in which I saw a scripture reference or someone saying a scripture. The night prior to writing this particular chronicle, I was approached in my dream. The person simply stated, "Isaiah 10" and that was it! Nevertheless, I knew it had to be God. Perhaps, it wouldn't be so obvious that it was God if there was no scripture reference. It was a response to a conversation that I'd just had with God, as I fell asleep that particular night. Moreover, I had multiple dreams that night to coincide with what I received spiritually from reading that chapter. But, wait! There's more!

Within that week, I had another dream in which someone gave me another chapter in the book of Isaiah to read. And in between these occurrences, during the one-week time frame, I'd been hearing various people reference the book of Isaiah. I decided to call the person who said "Isaiah 10" in my dream. I asked if this person had gotten a word regarding Isaiah 10, related to breakthroughs, burdens, and yokes. "That was the word during prayer when I attended church today!" is the response I received. Were the consistent references of I-sai-ah a coincidence?! I – say – uh… No!

63. This Means War!!!

Do you know the scripture that states to forget those things which are behind and press forward? Well, here's a great reason why you need to take heed, believe, adhere, and abide by that scripture: One day, I chose to dwell too much on "yesterday." I say "chose" because what we focus on is a matter of choice. Sometimes, it's easy to stay focused and other times, not so much. *(Note: Although it's not always easy, it's always possible.)* This particular day, it was not easy: It was a day that I needed to fight. I'd been wrestling mentally and emotionally for days.

I awakened with remnants of the previous day. I became exhausted and discouraged from the constant spiritual fight and battle to keep myself uplifted, with no encouragement from others. With nothing to hold onto and stand on, but my faith in God. Yet, I was tired of fighting to keep myself uplifted. Tired of stating the positive affirmations only to have the fulfillment of my requests prolonged. Tired of filling myself with the Word of God. Tired of praying. Tired of the transition I was in. Or am I being too real with you all? Maybe you can't relate. Whatever the case, this is my truth so I'm going to tell it.

I was just flat out exhausted. I was tired of watching the positive Periscope videos. Yet, "something" told me to tune in any way and well, well, well. The apostle spoke that when we're going to a new place, we don't get where God wants us without a fight, and when faith is hurt, you can't always just charge forward. Change must occur psychologically. As the broadcaster proceeded to give instructions about how to battle your way out, he said, "You have to fight!!...If you want to get to the blessing tomorrow, you have to fight and get past the curse of today!"

One by one, the man of God started naming the things that I was tired of waiting on. The fact that he was naming each element and explaining how to keep myself built up was not a coincidence. What's more is, I hadn't said my positive affirmations that morning (many of which are biblical scriptures and promises of God). Although the pastor didn't personally know me, or the things on my list, he started saying some of MY affirmations! One by one. As if he was intentionally reading my list:

- NO weapon formed against me shall prosper.
- Every tongue that rises up against me in judgment, I will condemn.
- I can do all things through Christ who strengthens me.
- He was wounded for my transgressions…by His stripes, I am healed.
- I commit my ways to the Lord and He gives me the desires of my heart.
- The blessings of the Lord make me rich and add no sorrow.

- I will be kept in perfect peace with my mind stayed on God.
- So shall my words be that go forth out of my mouth; they will not return to me void but will accomplish the purpose for which I send them.

He proceeded to explain that to achieve victory, I must discipline myself to believe The Word. Ironically enough, earlier in the prior day, I was meditating on Proverbs 19:20-21, "Listen to advice and accept discipline, and at the end you will be counted among the wise. Many are the plans in a person's heart, but it is the LORD's purpose that prevails."

I kept telling myself that I needed to be disciplined but somehow, later that day, I allowed myself to be mentally derailed. The memory of the pastor's admonishment earlier about being disciplined was pounding me on the head! Because I received the word to discipline myself and then the moment arose to apply what I'd listened to, it's as if God sent an answer just before the question. The advice I needed (from the Periscope video) to be disciplined and further meditate on the Word was God's ever-present help. I fought to hold back tears, as every arrow shot was penetrating my heart with love. All I could do was say: "Thank you Jesus" and then start speaking the heavenly language.

Can I give you another confession? Can you really handle my truth? Well, I'm telling it anyway. As much as God speaks to me, I still struggle and have sporadic moments of feeling like He's forgotten me. I know darn well He doesn't but sometimes, there are places that get so dark, I still have to fight like never before, even though I know the truth. I'm just showing you all that I'm not perfect either. I'm no more special to God than you are: That's proof that He talks to you just as He talks to me. Yet, during this particular "episode", I allowed myself to fall into a dark space. I say I allowed it because I should've immediately fallen on my face when I felt alone. But, I didn't so I contributed to my state of feeling alone.

Note: This is a reminder of what NOT to do and what happens when you DON'T pray. Prayer is filling and without it, you'll be running on empty.

Nonetheless, when I tuned into that scope with the man of God declaring my positive affirmations, I was fully persuaded it was the Holy Spirit who advised me to tune into Periscope and God used the apostle that morning! Prior to that scope, it's as if I was dry, but then someone poured an ocean of anointing deliverance, joy, and peace upon me! Even the best of us can have the worst of moments; but, during spiritual (emotional, mental, physical) battles, you have to fight! If you don't rise and fight to win, you will fall and lose! Remember, when the Devil attacks, "This means war!"

Note: Just because something isn't easy, doesn't mean it isn't possible.

64. Overflow

Jeremiah 29:11! "For I know the plans I have for you…plans to prosper you and not to harm you, plans to give you hope and a future." That was the scripture I chose to focus on. Then, a prophet mentioned it via a Periscope video, and he wasn't particularly talking to me. As the prophet proceeded, he mentioned Deuteronomy 1:11, which speaks about God increasing you a thousand times and blessing you as He has promised. This scripture seemed relevant; however, it was even more poignant for me because I'd been seeing 111 excessively within the preceding days. He referenced Exodus 34 and God entering a covenant and enlarging MY territory. Although I was only watching the prophet's video, wasn't communicating with him, and he wasn't particularly talking to me, I KNOW that message was for ME! How do I know? Well, I sowed a seed the previous day to enter into covenant with God for Him to increase my territory!

The prophet proceeded to say what Numbers 23:19 informs us: God is not a man that He should lie and once God tells me something, it means it's already done. As I was listening, I was inclined to check my email and what appeared before me in the commencement of an inspirational email was Psalm 139:16, "All the days ordained for me were written in your book before one of them came to be." Confirmation! God was informing and confirming that He'd already approved and written plans in my life, even before I was born into the physical realm.

What's even more exciting is the literature in the email! It stated, "He's written out plans for your good, plans to prosper you, plans for peace." Wow! It's as if Jeremiah 29:11 and Psalm 139:16 were combined into one sentence. Are you following me so far?

1. I chose to study Jeremiah 29:11 that day.
2. The prophet mentioned Jeremiah 29:11.
3. The prophet said when God tells you something, it's already done.
4. Then, I read Psalm 139:16 almost the same time the prophet was saying what the Psalm states.
5. Not only did the email reference 139:16 and how my days were already written, but it also had literature regarding what Jeremiah 29:11 states (although Jeremiah wasn't particularly referenced or written verbatim in the email).

6. And let's not forget the three ones (111),

7. Or how the prophet just so happened to mention the covenant and territory increasing! (I'd entered a covenant regarding increase the prior day.)

And guess what? There's more! As I was sitting at my desk with email still open on my laptop, and the Periscope broadcast still going, I glanced over to my right. On the right side of my desk, is where my Bible typically remains open on the last page that I was reading. It was still on Jeremiah and as I glanced over, my eyes met Jeremiah 29:10. I'd already been feeling that once I finish THIS BOOK, God was going to move in an unthinkable way! As my eyes met Jeremiah 29:10, I felt something in my spirit and it seemed that I read this verse differently from prior times. As I saw, "When 70…are completed…I will visit you and keep my promise!" I just KNEW that God was confirming that when I finish this book (70…, you're currently reading), He would fulfill what He'd already promised me.

And guess what? There's even more! As you can see, there was definitely an overflow of God's glory coming through so I started writing all that was occurring. As I was writing, the prophet stated, "God told me, 'If you do this, I'll do that.' OMG! Seriously?! I'd just read and felt God saying that if and when I finish this book, "70…" God will move and then the prophet confirmed it! These things were happening almost simultaneously! Had I not already known God as I did at that moment, surely I would've thought I was going insane.

Note: When God fills your cup, you CANNOT contain it. He sends an overflow that is truly over the top and unfathomable!

65. Call me XYZ

My cup was on overflow and still running over from some things God spoke to me the prior day. For some reason, a friend kept crossing my mind. I recalled the last conversation that she and I had. As we spoke, words flowed from my mouth to confirm revelations that she received from the Bible study she'd just left prior to our meeting for lunch. Although we were meeting at a restaurant to appease our carnal food appetites, she was losing her appetite for many things, losing the desire to converse about certain topics, losing the desire to watch television, etc. The overall epiphany is that she was in a transition of spiritual growth and maturity.

As I thought of her this particular morning, the word transition kept arising so, I decided to pray over her transition/spiritual growth, maturity and wisdom. I was so filled with the Holy Spirit, yet my stomach wasn't full at all. It continued to growl, and I could sense its anger increasing. I desired a healthy smoothie and had no more fresh fruit so I grabbed my phone to go to the store. As I picked it up, I noticed I had a message from the friend I'd just prayed for. This may not seem ironic, but she and I talk every few weeks, so to me, it was no coincidence that she texted me at that particular time. Anyway, I told her how I'd just finished praying over her and her transition and she replied, "Wow! I was just speaking to my husband about my transition!"

Isn't that amazing? Folks! I don't have any special powers or magic (unless you count the truth, light, and power of God that is revealed via the Holy Spirit)! God doesn't need to call you on a phone to talk to you. He has telekinetic power: He dials into and calls your spirit!!!

Note: Many times, when people cross our minds, it is because we should be praying over/for them (even your enemies)!

66. Standing Still is Moving

I'd written an Instagram post about seeking God first with questions and entering rest while waiting for Him to answer. That day (Day 1), I coincidentally received an email with Psalm 27:14 – "Wait for the Lord; be strong and take heart and wait for the Lord." The Instagram post was written without reading this message. The next day (Day 2), I received an email (from a different source than the email on the prior day) stating Exodus 14:13, 14 – "Do not be afraid. Stand firm and you will see the deliverance the Lord will bring you today…the Lord will fight for you; you need only to be still." Two emails and my Instagram post, all about resting and waiting for the Lord? At first, I paused and honestly thought of it as perhaps being a coincidence.

I stepped outside (on Day 2) just to put my thoughts on pause, breathe in fresh air, and observe nature. There was a subtle breeze; however, the temperature was perfect. The small tree limbs and leaves waved at me as they swayed back and forth. Then, suddenly, everything just halted. I thought it very strange how one minute everything seemed to be moving peacefully and in harmony. But, the next minute, everything froze. I looked around to ensure I wasn't going insane; I realized I was the only thing moving. Then I received a prophetic word: "Just as everything is standing still. This is how it's going to be for you. Everything is going to seem still, but you're still going to be moving."

The Revelation: *Even when I'm intentionally taking a moment to pause, it'll seem that things are still but my being still is actually going to be movement.*

At the time of receiving this revelation, I still didn't connect the dots regarding how God kept sending me these messages with the same punch line. Day 3, I was watching Joel Osteen when he said to seek God, not others, and ask when unsure or not feeling peace. He proceeded to talk about asking God for wisdom and *waiting* for Him to answer. This was exactly what I explained in the Instagram post (on Day 1). I also expressed that we should meet with and ask God before meeting with and asking other people, just as Joel said. The post I'd written started out as me attempting to encourage others, but I realized that God was obviously not just speaking through but also to me. He used me to encourage myself and I didn't even know it!

Even after all of that, I later stepped outside again (on Day 3) to breathe in nature and the experience of all of the above instances hit me! Three days!!! It took three days for me to put the pieces together! I'd previously perceived these instances as individual, autonomous occurrences. Yet, each individual segment (for the prior three days) fitted together and painted a picture that made sense. *(Note: It's not just a Bible scripture: All things really do work together for good for us!)*

Do you see how everything came together? I was able to recognize how pieces fitted together:

- When I turned the television off and talked to God
- When I decided to sit *still* in peace and quiet
- When I deliberately waited to hear God speak

The beautiful thing is how God kept affirming and confirming His revelation to me. It's as if He knocked and kept knocking until I opened my mind and spirit to the notice He was giving me. This is proof that there are times that when God wants you to get something, He'll keep coming after you until you receive it (Assuming your heart and spirit are open to Him). When people say God isn't a God of confusion, they are correct! He will send confirmation! So, if you don't get confirmation or if you get no answer at all, maybe, it's not God or you just need to be still and wait for an answer. Notice, I said "an answer." Make sure you're not open to just the answer that you want. Because if that's all you listen and look out for, you might miss the actual message that God sends.

Note 1: Sometimes, God is speaking through AND to you!

Note 2: Sometimes, being still is movement!

67. Get Ready...Get Ready...Get Ready...Get Ready!!!

Before I start, let me admonish you to read chronicle 66 (Standing Still is Movement), if you haven't already. It's sort of a precursor to this one. And if you haven't read it, what are you doing skipping chronicles? I'm just kidding. Read this book however you wish, just read it! (And of course, absorb and apply what you've learned). Now, we can begin chronicle 67.

After that 3rd day, I received an email that read, "See, the former things have taken place, and new things I declare; before they spring into being I announce them to you" (Isaiah 42:9). This would not be so poignant had I just not recently received various prophetic words from God about how my current state of being was actually movement for me. Not only did He announce how my present stance was related to my future, now, He was confirming that He made announcements to advise me of new, upcoming things to take place! What's more is that when I read the email, something inside of me jumped!

I immediately recalled how only days prior, a prophet stated that God will announce things to you prior to them happening. As you know, I can definitely testify to that, when I look back on many different experiences. I didn't think to associate the prophet's comment with the numerous times that God spoke to me and made me aware of things prior to them occurring. I was merely living and thinking in present times and even future times. And besides, I was still gloating over the revelation that I'd just received about standing still and *BOOM!* It's like all of these revelations hit me at once when I read Isaiah 42:9:

1. The prophet had just stated a few days ago that God announces things prior to them happening, and he wasn't reading the scripture in the Bible either. I didn't even know the words he was saying were an actual scripture (until this moment when it all hit me)!

2. God had just given me a revelation, advising me that standing still was actually movement. So, He gave me insight as to what was to come.

3. Now, He was confirming that what He'd been saying to me was indeed a word about what was to come. In addition, I felt strongly in my spirit that I definitely had a reason to be on the lookout.

4. Did you read chronicle #64 (about money coming one thousand fold)? That was one of the things revealed in very recent

days, (within the previous 7) but God had also been revealing things in my dreams!

I was already excited about the things God had been showing me. They were blowing my mind and hadn't even occurred in the natural yet. And then, here comes this scripture that I KNOW God sent! It's as if He was saying: Get ready. Get ready. Get ready. Get ready (in my Bishop T.D. Jakes' voice).

68. Fire, Where's Your Burn?

Have you ever been relaxing and didn't feel like being bothered but then someone felt the need to call you? Someone that you didn't particularly care to talk to? And although you weren't answering the phone, they just kept calling and calling and calling (with NO real purpose or urgent need)? That feeling right there! That feeling of relaxation and satisfaction being interrupted by irritation is what I was feeling (times one thousand)! All was going just fine in my life and yet, someone wanted to enter and interrupt it. Someone VERY UNATTRACTIVE seemed to have an interest in me and although I gave them no reason to continue this obsession, they held onto it and felt the need to ask others about me and try to play Inspector Gadget to obtain my contact information. I typically overlook these obsession issues that folks tend to have with me, but for whatever reason, I was feeling like enough is enough!

My personal philosophy is that if you knock on a person's door, call their phone, ask them on a date, throw a hook, etc. and they don't answer, show any interest, bite the hook, etc., you should keep it moving. But, this person seemed determined to figure a way to contact me. His mind was made up that he was going to make me talk to him. How hilarious is that for someone to think they can MAKE a person talk to or have feelings for them?! Can you say P-S-Y-C-H-O? Not only is it psycho, it's FURTHERMORE unattractive. A begging/stalking person lacks self-love, self-esteem, and self-confidence and no one (with good sense) wants a person that is any of the above.

As I continued to dwell on the unattractiveness and petty attempts of this person and how he seemed to have something wrong mentally, the thoughts were getting deeper. The way this person was doing certain things, it was apparent that he was plotting something. I was thinking about taking legal and other actions. The list of actions for me to take was getting longer and I was becoming more and more irritated with the thoughts I was giving to this situation. I struggled with trying to understand how a person could have so-called feelings for someone they truly don't even know! This was merely a case of obsession!

God had recently gotten rid of one obsessed man and here this other one was still trying to hunt me down! Nevertheless, I started praying, even as I felt the fire of anger burning in my chest. Suddenly, I received an inclination to check my email. OMG! Really?! How and why was this happening? What was really going on at that moment? And this email?

I was using all of my strength to fight against rage and then there was this! An email stating he cared for me and was watching me and everything occurring in my life! Seriously?! After receiving such an email, instead of becoming more furious, the fire was actually extinguished. As I continued to read, the email expounded upon how:

- God cares for me and sees every wrong that is done and plotted against me,

- He will vindicate and deliver me,

- He sees where I am and the struggles of my heart,
- He will pay me double for my trouble, and
- There's no need to be bitter, angry, or vengeful!

He gave me Psalm 31:7 and the more I read it aloud, the better I felt: "I will be glad and rejoice in your unfailing love, for you have seen my troubles, and you care about the anguish of my soul." How awesome is that?! The fire of anger was about to consume me, but God sent something as simple as an email to extinguish it!

Note: Some of you would've still been on fire and probably IN JAIL from choosing to do it your way, instead of God's way. When God sends help, accept it!

69. Never Alone

God will allow you to reach a place where you have no one to turn to (besides Him). People will be busy, bombarded, unavailable, and consumed with numerous things. This does not mean that you have no friends, no one cares, or no one loves you. It just means that God wants you to ultimately seek and use Him for your source of strength. I had to learn and convince myself of this. When I told my mother of a time I was wondering why she hadn't called, she reminded me and simply stated, "Just because a person does not call does not mean that they do not care." She was completely right. Besides, how could I expect a woman nearly sixty years of age who works six days per week, amongst other responsibilities to have time to call me, when I want her to call?

It's vital to remain logical and remember that we cannot always have what we want when we want it. To expect my mother to call just because I desired it was completely illogical and inconsiderate. Nevertheless, it was just a deeper yearning within me stemming from childhood that I still hadn't quite resolved. Unresolved issues led me to a declining moment when I felt like no one cared about the things concerning me. Suddenly, the phone rang and it was my best friend. I didn't want her to know about my depressed state, so I did not answer. A few hours later, the phone rang and it was my dad. I didn't want him to know about my depressed state either, so again, I didn't answer. Hours later, during an up moment, another friend texted that I had not talked to in weeks. She just wanted to check in and see how I was doing. The next day, my niece called just to say hello.

Do you see what God did? He knew I felt alone in this world and like no one knew I was alive. Everyone was consumed with their lives and no one cared about what I was going through, or at least, that is what I felt and thought at the time. Nevertheless, God refused to let me sit alone and believe that. But, wait! There's more! A few days later, I was starting to slump down into a dark moment when I was contacted by my aunt. She'd traveled to my city and surprised me with her visit. I immediately felt joy! Then, she took my child and me out to lunch, and we did not order cheap dishes! Because of the restaurant my aunt chose, we did not have a choice but to order meals that were costly. I tried to pay for my own meal but when I pulled out my card to pay our tab, my aunt said that she was taking care of the bill. At that moment, I felt another realm of joy! We stayed at the restaurant for four hours! It was one of the best surprise visits I'd gotten in a while.

God just keeps blessing me. He keeps me surrounded with people who are truly loving and supportive of me. Although I do not have to, that is a request that is perpetually in my prayers – being surrounded by loving people with serene spirits. It's definitely good to have those people in your life, but it's also good to be one of them. You never know how you might be touching another person. A person could be desperately in need of your kindness. Remember, there is always someone who could use your kind words, gestures or joyful appearance.

70. One Call Away

Who's the first person that you call when someone angers you and you need to calm down? Or when your check is short and you need to pay a bill before something gets cut off? Or when the doctor says the test results are abnormal, so they need to run more tests to see if it's XYZ? Or when your significant other has tried you with some foolishness? Or when your children are trying to get out of control? Or when you find out another friend has actually turned out to be an enemy? Or when you're just tired of the merry-go-round of not really being happy and things rarely consistently going right? Or when you're just tired of feeling like you're fighting through life alone? Or when you're discouraged and confused about why your life just doesn't get on the right track? Who do you call?

Perhaps, it's one person that you can really trust. It might even be several different people. For me, it used to be several different people. That is, until God started causing people to be unavailable during a time in my life when I was holding on with my last bit of breath. At the time, that is precisely what it felt like — breathing was becoming difficult. Every single day (and this is no exaggeration), something was going wrong in my life. It was the time when the doctor said that I was at risk for going completely blind. It was also the time that my car was flooded and I'd just started a new second job. I had to miss time (and needed money), already. It was the time when my job contract had ended for my primary bread-winner, and I couldn't get another assignment. The list goes on and on.

I'd reached the point where I hated going to sleep because I only had nightmares about the calamities that were hitting my life. I hated waking up because there was a new abnormal challenge every day. During that stretch of time, I just couldn't understand what was going on. Did I commit some horrible sin that I hadn't repented of? Was I some low-down, evil villain and somehow didn't know it? Was God mad at me? Was God hearing me or was He just ignoring me? Had God forgotten me? Just as the list of issues seemed infinite, so were my questions.

Eventually, I became enraged! I was furious and excessively livid. How could God keep allowing so many things to happen to me? I was a good person. I had never been perfect, but I'd been deepening my relationship with Him like never before for a few years at that point. Why was He forsaking me? Had I gone mad? Maybe, every time I had communication with God before, it was just my imagination. Where was He? Was He real?

Friend, I was about to seriously lose my mind. And to top it all off, I was in a fight by myself. It's not that no one wanted to help me. They were just unavailable. In addition, I also became so exhausted and depressed that most days, I didn't even feel like explaining all of my bad luck news. I reached a point where I basically woke up, went to work (at a job that couldn't pay my bills), came home, cried myself to sleep and repeat. But then, one day! One day, I let out all of my anger and frustration. To God! As I called myself, questioning Him and asking why my life was always filled with such abnormal trial periods, "somebody got told off"!

Yes, I thought I was giving Him a piece of my mind — until!!! Until I heard His voice clearly! He spoke in an aggressive, disapproving manner that I'm not really sure how to explain. All I know is that I immediately humbled myself because I suddenly felt extremely fearful. Nevertheless, He and I had an extensive conversation. By the time we were done, I knew to study the book of Job.

Everybody knows the very short, condensed version of the story of Job, but I'd never studied it, until then. After my conversation with God and studying the book of Job, I felt a way I hadn't felt in about six months. I still had problems, but I felt hopeful and encouraged. Although I couldn't see the entire big picture, God had put many pieces of the puzzle together for me. For a few more weeks, the issues were still arising on a consistent basis. Instead of my circumstances changing — I changed. When another issue arose, I would say, "God, you see this, right? I need you to handle this for me." When I said that prayer, I would proceed with my day as if my life was perfect and everything was in order. After a few weeks of that, suddenly, things started to change — one by one. It's as if I was so close to hitting rock bottom that I could actually taste pavement. Yet, just before I smashed into it, God stopped me and held me in that position for a while. Then, he slowly started bringing me back up.

Out of all the things I went through, during that pressing time, it was all for me to learn a lesson: to trust God! It's not that I didn't trust Him before, or at least I thought I did. When I started going through the fire, it revealed that I didn't trust Him like I thought I did. The level of trust, I had before the fire, needed to go to an entirely different level. That scorching trial truly was painful, but I say in all honesty, it was good for me that I was afflicted.

The level of trust and faith I have in Him today is on a level like never before BECAUSE of that sweltering time period in my life. A time period when no one else could rescue me from the dungeon I was in. In fact, when I needed money for eye surgery and glasses, someone actually helped me. However, even if they helped with one predicament, they couldn't have possibly helped with all. I would've easily stressed out others if they had to help me every single day with every single dilemma that was coming my way. It's awesome to have friends and family who can and will help us. Like I asked at the beginning of this chronicle, who do you call? We all need friends and family at some point, but God is who we need overall, first and foremost. So now, when I have any sort of dilemma, He is the first one I call!

BONUSES

71. Speak Lord, Your Servant is Listening

I have countless experiences regarding on-time emails from various unrelated resources, who just so happen to expound on the same scriptures and messages, around the same time period. Here's one: One day I received emails from two sources. Both were referencing Matthew 7:7-8 telling us to ask and keep asking, seek and keep seeking. These emails appeared to be a response to a request to God. I'd submitted my request and had been waiting and wondering what the next step would be. I asked God if there was something more for me to do. And voila! This scripture reference couldn't have given clearer directions than this!

Note: Talk to God: He talks back!

72. The Bible Knows

As you can guess by this point, I've opened my Bible and it just happened to be on a very relevant scripture that was extremely applicable at the time of reading. As a matter of fact, there was a moment when someone reached out to me, needing a word. After speaking through the Spirit to this person, I opened the Bible and guess what? My Bible was being prophetic. LOL. For real! It was where it needed to be and pretty much perfectly summed up the word I'd just given. With that being said, you know I had to send that scripture to them. It's amazing how Holy Spirit shows up and shows out! Or was all this just a coincidence? To anyone who wants to say this was a coincidence, please make sure you spell it as c-o-n-f-i-r-m-a-t-i-o-n! ☺

73. **Praise for Prayer**

I was sipping (liquor) and it wasn't as appealing to my tongue as usual. I frowned and spoke about how something wasn't right. Then, my mother said, "I prayed for God to take that taste away from you." OMG! Seriously?! I started thinking, "Why is this lady trying to punish me?!" LOL. I guess I was loving the taste so much that I didn't have enough sense to pray that prayer for myself; so, someone else was praying it for me.

I still tried to "go against the grain" even after that and tried to force myself to continue drinking liquor. My desire wasn't completely dead, and I was trying to keep alive the little drop I had. However, somewhere along the way, I suddenly lost interest in drinking liquor. It's like I woke up one day and just felt that it was pointless to drink like I'd drank formerly. I used to actually have an appetite for liquor, the same way that people yearn for desserts. Thanks to my mom, not only did I lose the taste (literally), but I lost the desire. Praise God for people who pray "for" you!

74. **Who Am I Serving?**

I'd started a new job. This was during the time when God was finally putting things in my life back into place, one-by-one. I was ecstatic that instead of waking up to a new issue, I was waking up to a new good thing, daily. I was enjoying meeting new people and one lady was very nice and cool. That is, until she started talking more and more about all this "Egyptian stuff" and how Jesus isn't real. Some of the things she said seemed to make sense, and I honestly started getting confused.

During lunch break, I sat in my car and talked to God. I explained the situation and dilemma. I told Him I was becoming confused. Had I been serving the wrong God all that time? He'd spoken to me countless times throughout my life; it seemed like He would've already told me if I was serving incorrectly. If God could tell me the many things He'd told me throughout the years, surely, He would've told me that! I concluded my prayer and checked my email. At this moment, I think I can stop writing this chronicle because I know you already know where this is going. So, I'm done!

Thanks for taking the time to read my testimonies. Have a great day! LOL. You know I can't do you like that. Although you can tell me what happened, I'm going to confirm it for you. So, as I opened my email, there it was! I had another one of those daily inspirational, spiritual emails. The email said to just stay focused on Jesus! Okay, I'm done! ☺

HEAVENLY NOTES

- God sends warnings. Lookout and listen.
- When the Spirit touches you, it is more than a feeling and facts always follow.
- Sometimes, we don't know what we need, but God always does. Just because you don't know how you'll get what you need, doesn't mean you won't get it.
- Silence isn't golden if God gives you the words to speak. Those words are worth a lot more than gold.
- Sometimes, what it takes is for you to pray, speak a word of faith, and be highly convinced that the thing you speak is going to occur. It's cool to believe and expect, but you need to KNOW.
- Seek and you shall find.
- You have power that you aren't aware of and therefore aren't using.
- Just before everything goes down, God will stop it.
- Sometimes, God's messages are not even as deep as you might think. They might be simply simple and a matter of you paying just a little attention — enough attention to recognize patterns.
- Pay Him attention and there's no limit to what He'll pay you.
- Don't spend a lot of time trying to do what God can do in seconds.

- You don't need them to believe in you. You just need to believe in you.
- Talk to God: He's listening.
- God shines light on darkness.
- Your story is more for others than yourself. Don't be selfish—share.
- Just because we don't see things happening in the physical, it doesn't mean they aren't already done.
- If the Devil can stop you, he can stop others from getting what they need.
- Even if you "fail", you can still excel "pass" it.
- When frustration blurs your vision, adjust your focus. It's not your sight, it's what you're looking at.
- Seek God and do not lean to your own understanding.
- Not only does God speak to us regarding us, but He gives us knowledge and wisdom for others too.
- Prayer is filling and without it, you'll be running on empty.
- Just because something isn't easy, doesn't mean it isn't possible.
- When God fills your cup, you CANNOT contain it. He sends an overflow that is truly over the top and unfathomable.
- Many times, when people cross our minds, it is because we should be praying over/for them (even your enemies).

- It's not just a Bible scripture; all things really do work together for good for us.
- Sometimes, God is speaking through AND to you.
- Sometimes, being still is movement.
- When God sends help, accept it.
- God is always there. Your lack of His awareness does not negate His presence.
- Talk to God: He talks back.

A WORD OF ENCOURAGEMENT

God loves you and cares about every miniscule and enormous thing in your life (and everything in between). One time, I started seeing bugs in my home and freaked out so badly that I prayed for God to get rid of them. Funny right? But, they finally disappeared. Things that may seem too stupid to pray about, pray about them! If you can think about them, you can and should pray about them. God doesn't have a stupid-smart scale when it comes to prayer. Unfortunately, sometimes, we judge God based on people. But, God isn't like people. The things people judge us about, God does not. He is more concerned than judgmental. So, don't hesitate to talk to Him anytime, about anything.

If you've already been speaking to God, speak more and if you've never, then start. We don't always need apostles, prophets, evangelists, pastors, and teachers to speak to or even get a word from God for us. We can get it ourselves. Of course, these people are still important and needed, but we shouldn't always primarily depend on them for a word from the Lord. Besides, why wait on someone else to deliver a word from God to you when you can get it yourself. Furthermore, many times, God has already told you something but you weren't listening or you didn't know it was Him. *Missing a word from God could cause you to miss an opportunity.* Surely, you don't want that! That's why you must seek and lean on God.

Lean on and trust in the Lord. In other words, depend on Him for support and put your hope in Him and His power. Rely confidently on Him with all your heart (no half-stepping) not on your own understanding. Your own understanding is mixed with human emotions, which are often flawed. In all your ways (meaning behaviors, habits, all you do, etc.), know, acknowledge, and recognize Him, and He'll direct your paths (Proverbs 3:5-6). There it is! That's one of the main reasons you need to know how to hear God: He will direct your paths, but you must know, acknowledge, and recognize Him. And how exactly can you ensure that you are doing all three?

- Know Him — Build a relationship. Spend time to accomplish this. Spending time leads to intimacy.

- Acknowledge Him — Seek Him for advice and direction. Talk to Him about what's going on: big, small, questions, giving thanks, casual expressions, praise, worship.

- Recognize Him — This, you can do when intimacy is established.

When you do these, He will direct your path. He will make it straight and plain (meaning evident and obvious). "Straight" doesn't mean the road won't ever be crooked, and you won't experience bumps along the way. To make your path straight means to put it in alignment with His will, purpose, and plan for your life. You don't have to be confused about which way to go and what to do. And if for some reason, you're still confused, you should consult with Him because God is not a God of confusion. The messages shouldn't be mixed. If confusion is involved, it may not be God or you might just be missing something. God is a God of confirmation. Nevertheless, you must talk to Him and trust Him throughout the process.

There are some times when He may be silent; but, silence doesn't equate to absence. When unsure, it may be better to stand still until you know for sure what God wants you to do. On the other hand, if God has impressed a desire in your spirit (not necessarily including your mind), then it may be a time of testing for you to take a leap of faith. Just verify that it's God, as in Jesus Christ, who is telling you to either stand still or leap. Pray Psalm 25:4-5 to God and ask for confirmation. God can and will confirm whether you should stand still or leap.

God's Word is a lamp to guide your feet and a light for your path (Psalm 119:105), so make sure you read and study it. Your spirit is also a lamp from God because it is a source and device used to reveal light. The Holy Spirit will tap directly into your spirit and shine light on dark paths. When it's dark, it's hard to see where you're going. Have you ever been excited to travel to a place that you'd never been? And you didn't know the exact directions, but you were still excited? Because it was a foreign place to you, you might have even gotten lost once you got on the road, especially before GPS systems were popular. You were probably primarily depending on MapQuest. While being confused, you might've kept trying to find the place on your own, but eventually had to start asking questions and seeking additional help to find your way. Right? That's exactly how life can be.

We tend to try to find our way on our own. We think we have enough sense to figure things out, so at first, we keep trying and trying. Then, when we get too lost and become frustrated, we ask God for directions. But, what good is it to go and then ask which way to go? Doesn't it make more sense to ask which way to go first, and then go that way?

I admonish you to apply your newly found knowledge and ask God for instructions, so you can know which way to go and how (mode of travel so-to-speak) to get there. With that being said, you should increase your excitement just knowing that you're going to a new place in your life. Believe God to take you places you've never been and have only dreamed of (up until this point). Don't forget to use your GPS to get there. From this point on, you will be using the GPS (as in God's Perfect System) or at least, I hope you will. And even if God tells you where you're going, but doesn't give directions immediately, still be excited! Be excited to discover a new place, even prior to the GPS clearly mapping out the way.

It's not always easy, but it's always possible to get excited, in the midst of what feels like complete darkness, doom and gloom. You have to fight through those dark moments and build yourself up. Even when it feels like:

- You're all alone
- No one understands
- No one cares
- No one is listening
- No one knows (what you're going through)
- Nothing is working out
- It's taking too long
- You're tired
- Everything is dark

Even in darkness, light still exists. God is present and He knows, understands, cares, and is listening. Talk to Him — He talks back.

ABOUT ME

I have a Master of Science Degree in Human Services, but much of my wisdom, knowledge, and understanding of life has been acquired by actually living life. Education is a good teacher, but life is the best one. I strove alone for numerous years to overcome battles of depression, defeated thinking, low self-confidence, low self-esteem, and suicidal ideologies. During those moments, I was confused about life, my purpose, people, and everything else in between. It seemed that nothing in my life was consistent but my confusion, frustration, and depression.

I'd always (since elementary school) had a relationship with God. In fact, I was about seven or eight years of age when I got saved and also baptized. Of course, I prayed and went to church sporadically within my years of darkness. I was good to people and yet, to no avail, it seemed like I was still always struggling or suffering. Therefore, I understand dark places. God allowed darkness because the more darkness I was exposed to, the brighter a light shined.

I didn't learn about communicating with God or hearing Him by choice. I was forced. Well, actually it's a little of both. I had nowhere or no one to turn to. I'm not sure if it was the hole in my heart from always being misunderstood, disliked, mistreated, and rejected. Or the lack of happiness and consistent depression episodes. Or the confusion about who I was and what my purpose was. Or the always suffering or struggling with something "factor." Or maybe, all of the above is what forced me to delve ever so deep into my relationship with God, like I'd never done before. It's not because I was just bored, had nothing to do or decided upon an altar call.

I needed something desperately because my head was spinning so hard so fast; I was finally and ultimately drained like I'd never been drained before. I think each dark period just kept pushing me closer and closer to the point where I would have no choice but to seek answers, like never before. Ultimately, I had questions for too long and I desperately needed answers.

After the last extremely dark period in my life, a light came on, and I somehow entered into a new realm of knowing and understanding God. It just came with a pruning process by which He had to shave a lot of things off me so my channels would be unclogged. Ever since the channels have been unclogged, my antenna has tuned into an unbelievable frequency of supernatural wisdom, understanding, and knowledge. Ironically, it was always available to me. *God was always there. My lack of His awareness, did not negate His presence.* He was always guiding my forefront and cumulative in my background.

My background has led me to and through many places and spaces, good and bad. Nevertheless, my experiences, wisdom, understanding, and knowledge have led me to my current stand point and now I stand to teach and lead others, as well as help others to lead. I write to educate, motivate, and facilitate self-love, healing, and growth. In addition, I write as a form of therapy via poetry. Stay connected to me for updates!

- Subscribe to my email list for updates: www.1UniqueWriter.com.
- Follow me @1UniqueWriter on social media for daily/weekly motivation:
    - Instagram, Twitter, Facebook, YouTube, Periscope
- Other Books:
    - Find Your Purpose, 7-Step Challenge
    - Winning, 30 Days of Motivational Poetry

www.ingramcontent.com/pod-product-compliance
Lightning Source LLC
Chambersburg PA
CBHW021131300426
44113CB00006B/386